CONFIGURING INVENTORY MANAGEMENT WITHIN DYNAMICS AX 2012

BY MURRAY FIFE

ISBN-10: 1511838264

ISBN-13: 978-1511838269

Preface

What You Need For This Guide

All the examples shown in this blueprint were done with the Microsoft Dynamics AX 2012 virtual machine image that was downloaded from the Microsoft Customer Source or Partner Source site. If you don't have your own installation of Microsoft Dynamics AX 2012, you can also use the images found on the Microsoft Learning Download Center or deployed through Lifecycle Services. The following list of software from the virtual image was leveraged within this guide:

• Microsoft Dynamics AX 2012 R3

Even though all the preceding software was used during the development and testing of the recipes in this book, they may also work on earlier versions of the software with minor tweaks and adjustments, and should also work on later versions without any changes.

Errata

Although we have taken every care to ensure the accuracy of our content, mistakes do happen. If you find a mistake in one of our books—maybe a mistake in the text or the code—we would be grateful if you would report this to us. By doing so, you can save other readers from frustration and help us improve subsequent versions of this book. If you find any errata, please report them by emailing editor@blindsquirrelpublishing.com.

Piracy

Piracy of copyright material on the Internet is an ongoing problem across all media. If you come across any illegal copies of our works, in any form, on the Internet, please provide us with the location address or website name immediately so that we can pursue a remedy.

Please contact us at legal@blindsquirrelpublishing.com with a link to the suspected pirated material.

We appreciate your help in protecting our authors, and our ability to bring you valuable content.

Questions

You can contact us at help@blindsquirrelpublishing.com if you are having a problem with any aspect of the book, and we will do our best to address it.

Table Of Contents

INTRODUCTION

The Inventory Management area of Dynamics AX allows you to track all of the inventory within your warehouses, manage all of the movements and inventory adjustments and also set the inventory policies for costing. This is also the foundation for the other modules like Procurement & Sourcing and Sales Order Management because it gives you something to receive into and also ship from which is useful to track.

In this guide we will step you through the setup of all of the basic configuration that is needed in order to get your sites and warehouses configures, show you how to tweak your products so that they can be used within the warehousing structures, how to perform common inventory transactions like cycle counts and also how to configure batch controlled and serialized items.

CONFIGURING INVENTORY MANAGEMENT CONTROLS

Before we start setting up our warehouses and counting our inventory, there are a couple of codes and controls that we need to set up. These include item groups, costing controls, and inventory journals that will help us manage and move the products.

In this section we will help you get all of the housekeeping out of the way before we start with modelling and management of the inventory.

Configuring Item Groups

The first thing that we need to do is configure a set of Item Groups. These are pretty important, because they are not just used for classifying the different products, they also manage all of the default posting profiles for the products.

Configuring Item Groups

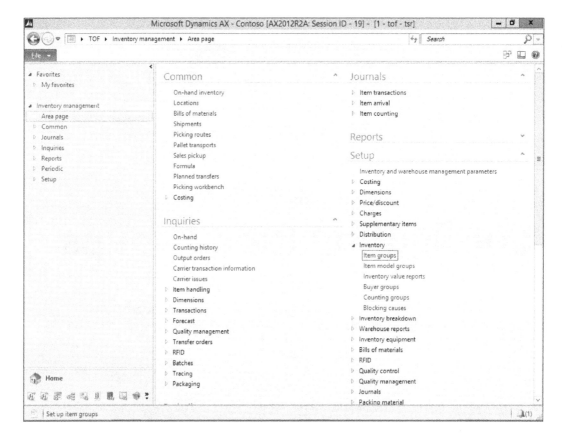

To do this click on the **Item Groups** menu item within the **Inventory** folder of the **Setup** group within the **Inventory Management** area page.

Configuring Item Groups

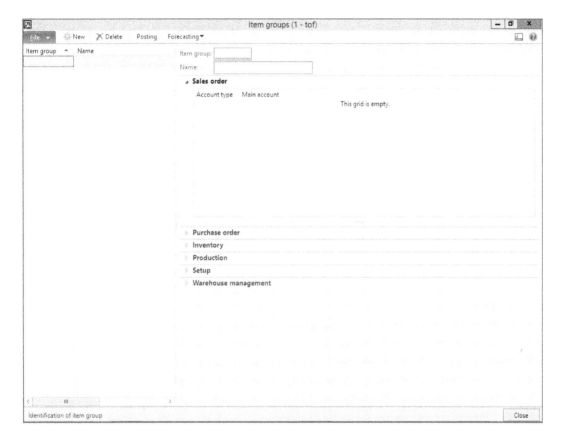

When the **Item Groups** maintenance form is displayed, click on the **New** button in the menu bar to create a new record.

Configuring Item Groups

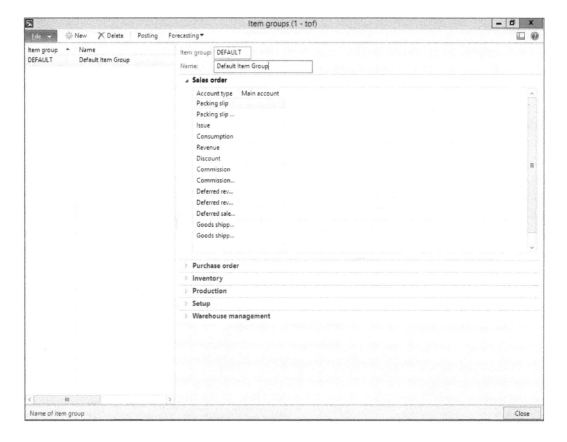

We will just create a generic item group for now as a catch all, so set the **Item Group** to **DEFAULT** and the **Name** to **Default Item Group.**

Then press **CTRL+S** to save the record. After you have done that, you will notice that a number of default account placeholders are populated in all of the child tab groups. These are the default Main Accounts that you can define to manage the postings for all items that belong to this group. You don't have to fill in them all, but you do have to set up quite a few in order to make sure everything runs smoothly.

Configuring Item Groups

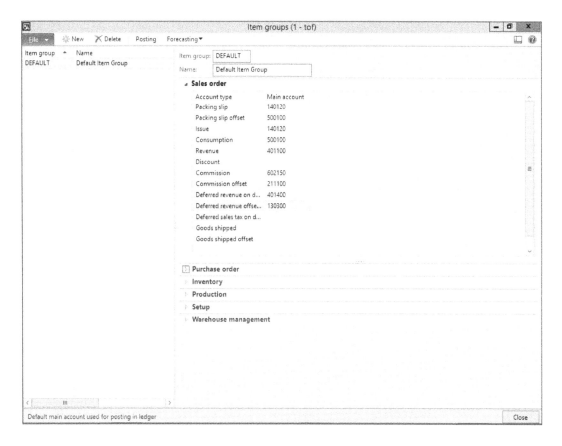

Start off within the **Sales Order** tab group and assign the following Account Types a Main Account.

Packing Slip	**120120**
Packing Slip Offset	**500100**
Issue	**140120**
Consumption	**500100**
Revenue	**401100**
Commission	**602150**
Commission Offset	**211100**
Deferred Revenues on d...	**401400**
Deferred Revenue offset	**130300**

Configuring Item Groups

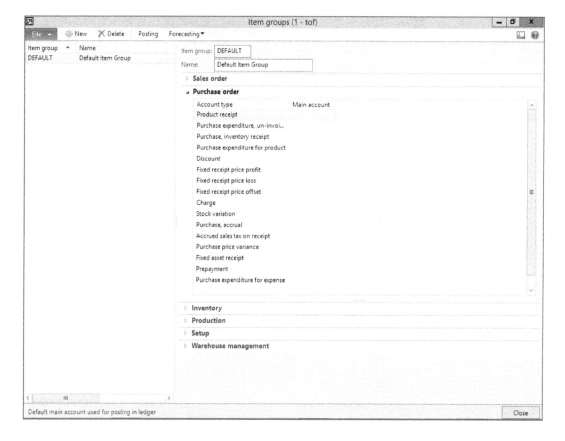

Now switch to the **Purchase Order** tab and you will see more accounts.

Configuring Item Groups

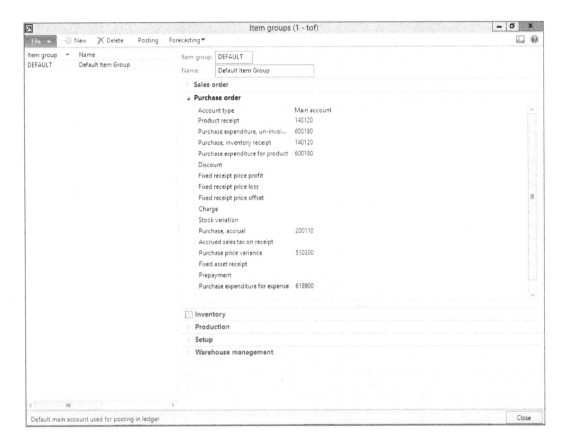

Assign the following Account Types a Main Account.

Product Receipt	**140120**
Purchase Expenditure un-invoices	**600180**
Purchase, inventory receipt	**140120**
Purchase expenditure for product	**600180**
Purchase Accrual	**200110**
Purchase Price Variance	**510300**
Purchase expenditure for expense	**618900**

Configuring Item Groups

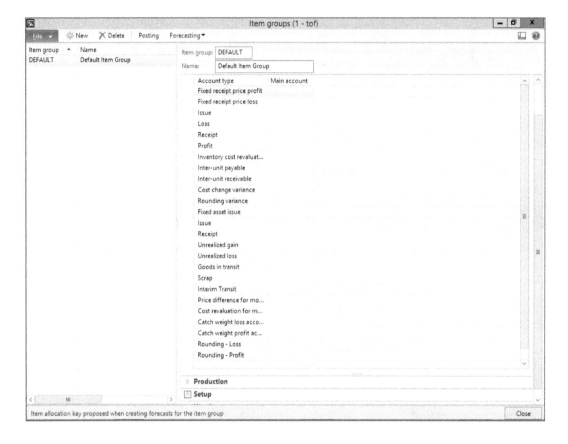

Now switch to the **Inventory** tab.

Configuring Item Groups

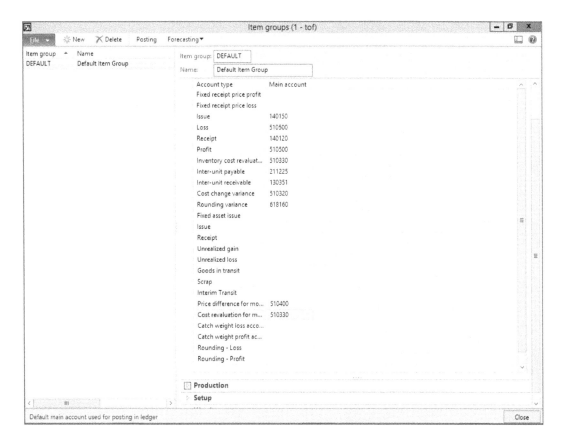

Assign the following Account Types a Main Account.

Issue	**140150**
Loss	**510500**
Receipt	**140120**
Profit	**510500**
Inventory Cost Revaluation	**510330**
Inter-unit Payable	**212225**
Inter-unit Receivable	**130351**
Cost Change Variance	**510320**
Rounding Variance	**618160**
Price Difference for m...	**510400**
Cost Revaluation for m...	**510330**

Configuring Item Groups

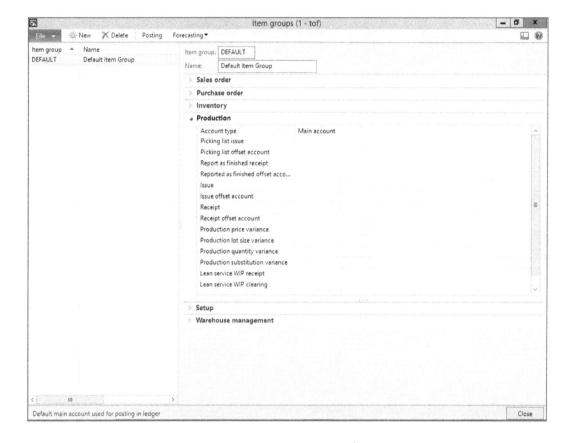

Finally switch to the **Production** tab.

Configuring Item Groups

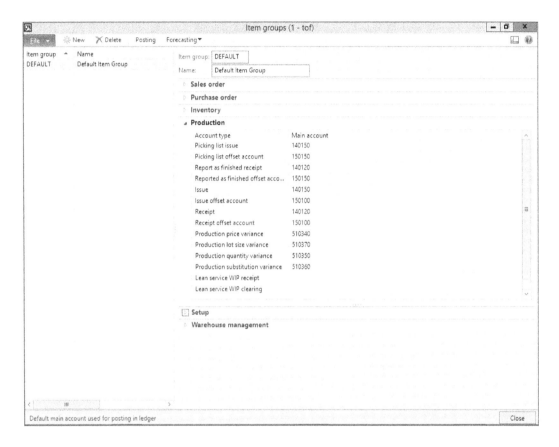

Assign the following Account Types a Main Account.

Picking List Issue	**140150**
Picking List Offset Account	**150150**
Report As Finished Receipt	**140120**
Reported as Finished Offset Account	**150150**
Issue	**140150**
Issue Offset Account	**150100**
Receipt	**140120**
Receipt Offset Account	**150100**
Production Price Variance	**510340**
Production Lot Size Variance	**510370**
Production Quantity Variance	**510350**
Production Substitution Variance	**510360**

Configuring Item Groups

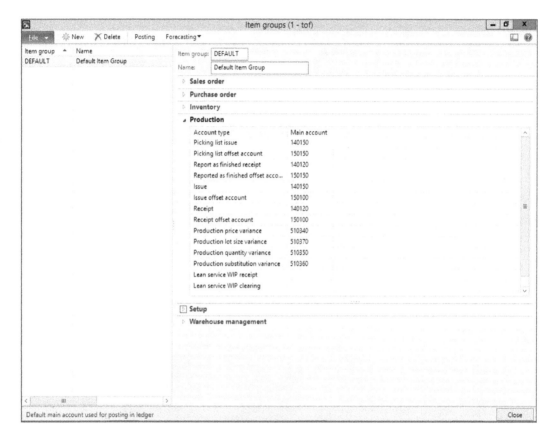

You can continue adding more Item Groups if you like and when you are done just click on the **Close** button to exit from the form.

Configuring Item Model Groups

Next we will want to configure your **Item Model Groups**. These tell the system how the items are going to be costed, and also have a lot of flags attached to them that allow you to tweak the way that the items are managed within the inventory.

Configuring Item Model Groups

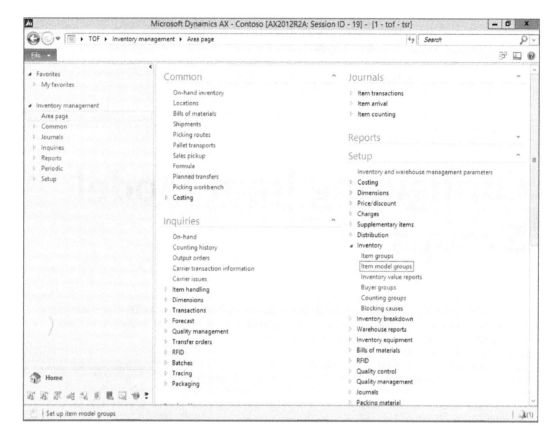

To do this, click on the **Item Model Groups** menu item within the **Inventory** folder of the **Setup** group within the **Inventory Management** area page.

Configuring Item Model Groups

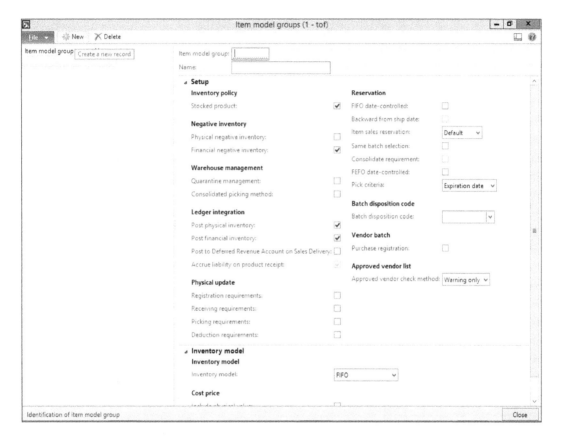

When the **Item Model Groups** maintenance form is displayed, click on the **New** button in the menu bar to create a new record.

Configuring Item Model Groups

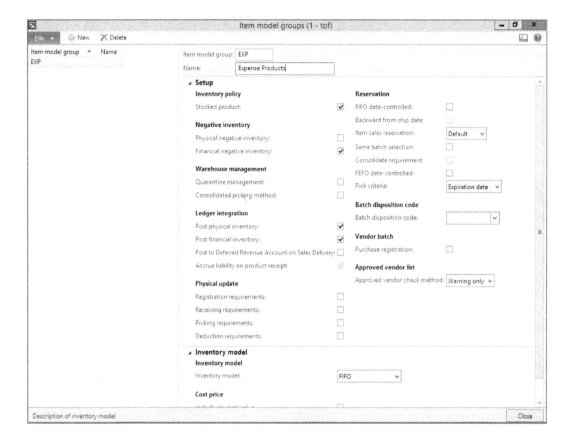

The first **Item Model Group** that we will set up is for expensed items, so set the **Item Model Group** code to **EXP** an the **Name** to **Expense Products**.

Configuring Item Model Groups

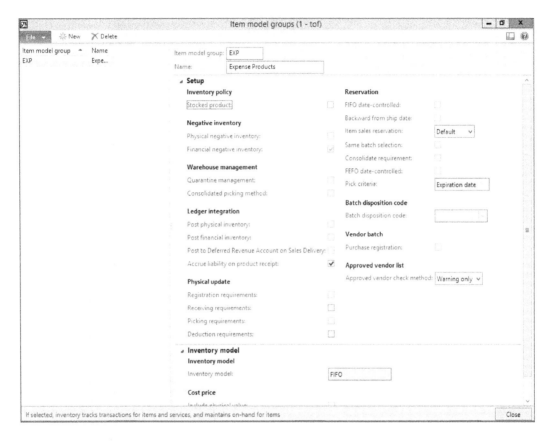

Since the expensed items will not be inventoried, uncheck the **Stocked Product** flag on the record and you are done.

Configuring Item Model Groups

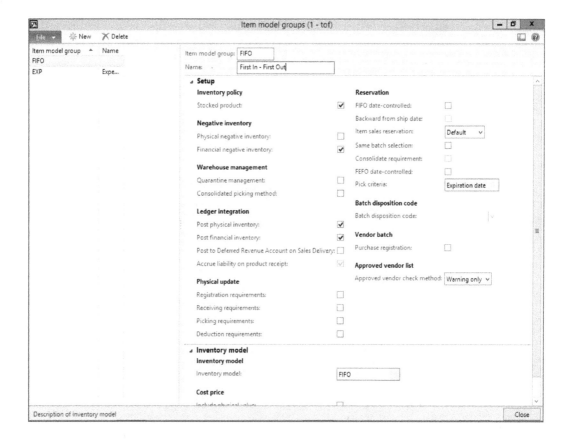

Now click on the **New** button in the menu bar to create a new record and set the **Item Model Group** code to **FIFO** and the **Name** to **First In – First Out.**

Configuring Item Model Groups

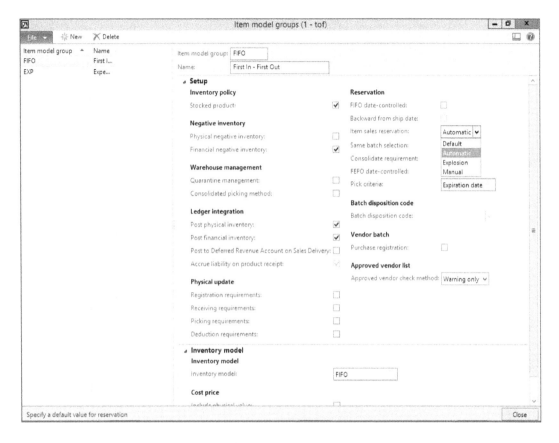

Within the **Reservation** field group, click on the **Item Sales Reservation** dropdown and select the **Automatic** option. This tells the system to automatically reserve the inventory at the time of order entry, which saves a lot of additional work later on.

Configuring Item Model Groups

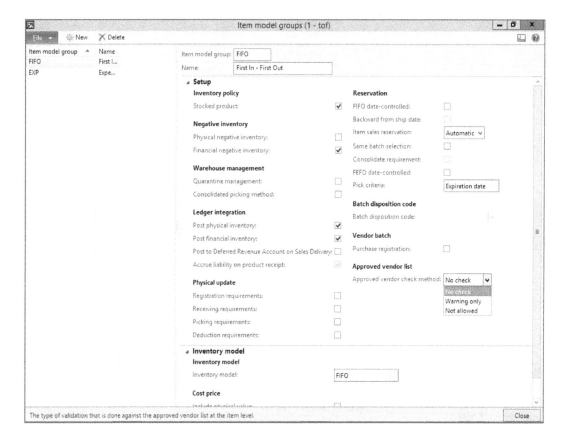

Also, to simplify your life, click on the **Approved Vendor Check Method** dropdown and select the **No Check** option. This will stop the system from checking if the vendor is an approved vendor when you create purchase orders which will streamline your setup just a little for now.

Configuring Item Model Groups

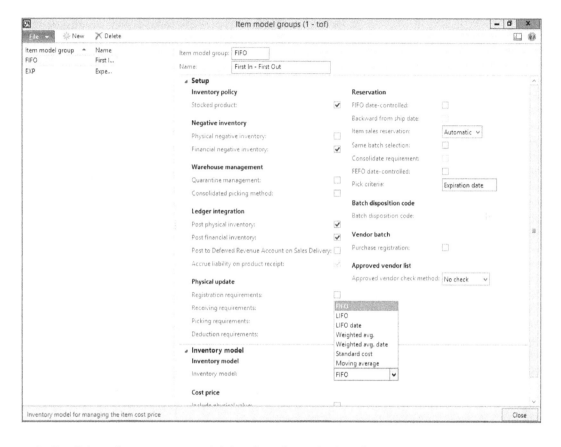

Finally, click on the **Inventory Model** dropdown list and select the **FIFO** model. Notice all of the other models that are there – we will set up some more of those next.

Configuring Item Model Groups

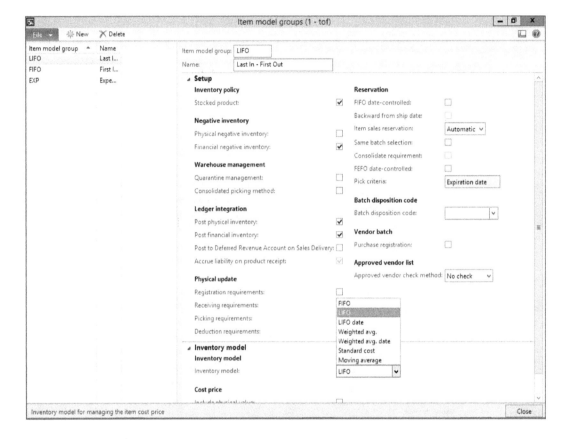

Click on the **New** button in the menu bar to create a new record and set the **Item Model Group** code to **LIFO** and the **Name** to **Last In – First Out**. Then set the **Item Sales Reservation** to **Automatic** and the **Approved Vendor Check Method** to **No Check**. Finally set the **Inventory Model** to **LIFO**.

Configuring Item Model Groups

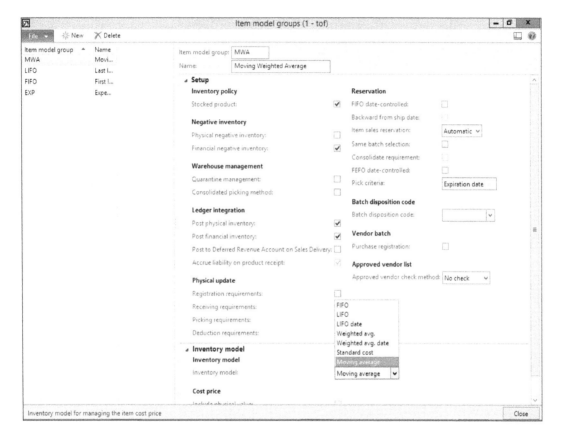

Click on the **New** button in the menu bar to create a new record and set the **Item Model Group** code to **MWA** and the **Name** to **Moving Weighted Average**. Then set the **Item Sales Reservation** to **Automatic** and the **Approved Vendor Check Method** to **No Check**. Finally set the **Inventory Model** to **Moving Average**.

Configuring Item Model Groups

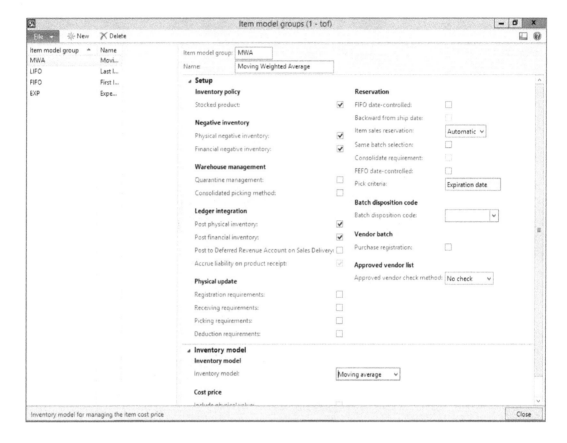

For this record though also check the **Physical Negative Inventory** flag within the **Negative Inventory** field group.

Configuring Item Model Groups

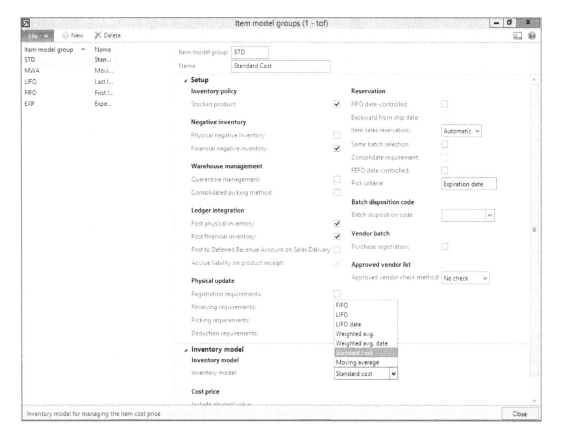

Click on the **New** button in the menu bar to create a new record and set the **Item Model Group** code to **STD** and the **Name** to **Standard Cost**. Then set the **Item Sales Reservation** to **Automatic** and the **Approved Vendor Check Method** to **No Check**. Finally set the **Inventory Model** to **Moving Average**.

Configuring Item Model Groups

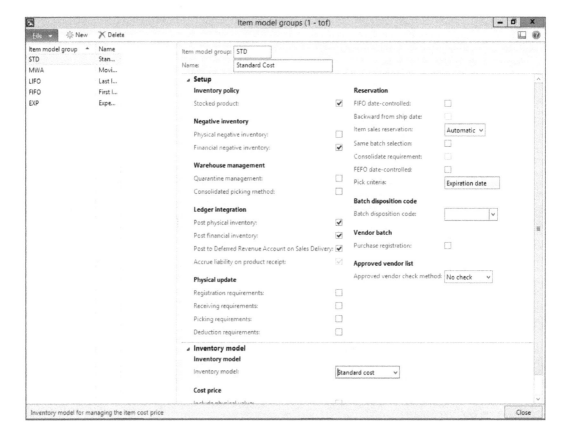

For this record also check the **Post Deferred Revenue Account On Sales Delivery** flag within the **Ledger Integration** field group.

These should be enough for now, so when you are done, click on the **Close** button to exit from the form.

Configuring Costing Versions

Next we want to set up some **Costing Versions** which we can start tracking product costs against. You can have many costing versions as you like within Dynamics AX and use them at different times depending on how you want to build up costs and prices, and you can keep separate costing versions within the system for planning and comparisons.

Configuring Costing Versions

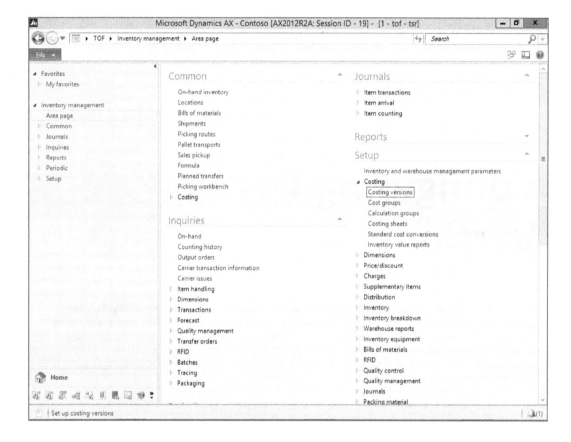

To do this, click on the **Costing Versions** menu item within the **Costing** folder of the **Setup** group within the **Inventory Management** area page.

Configuring Costing Versions

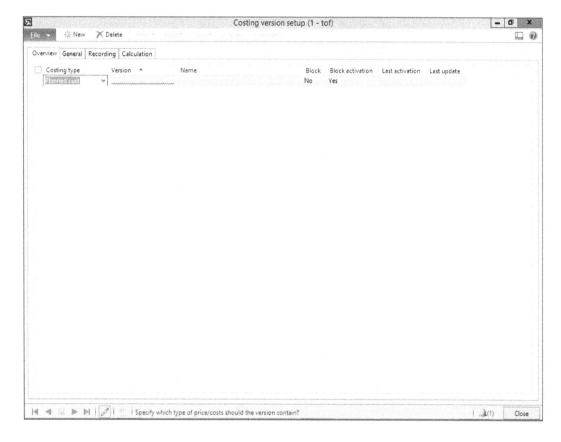

When the **Costing Version Setup** maintenance form is displayed, click on the **New** button in the menu bar to create a new record.

Configuring Costing Versions

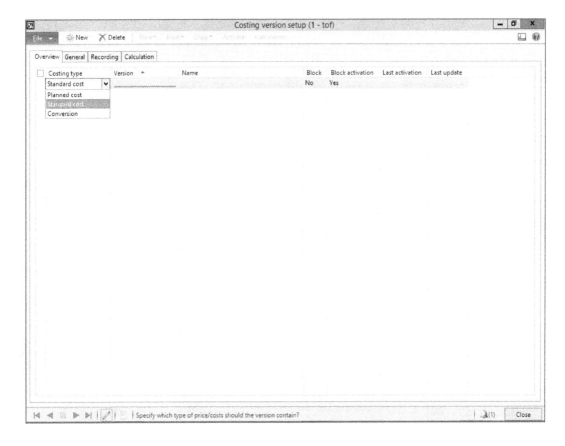

The first **Costing Version** that we will set up will be to track the standard costs. So click on the **Costing Type** dropdown list and select the **Standard Cost** value.

Configuring Costing Versions

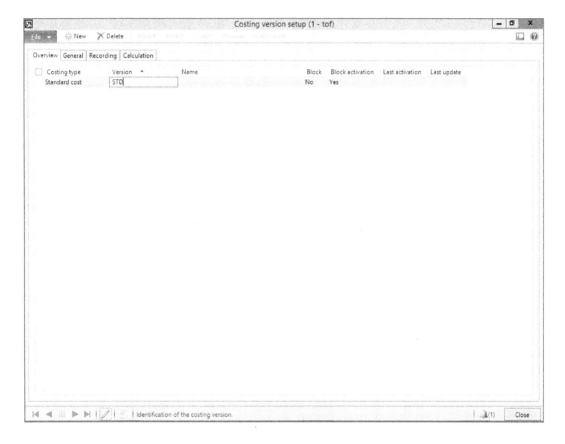

Then set the **Version** code to **STD**.

Configuring Costing Versions

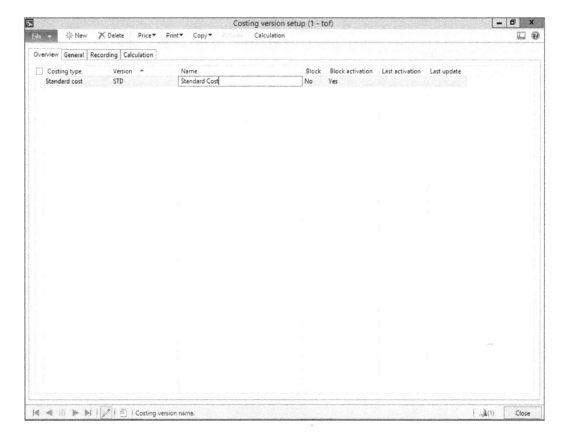

And then set the **Name** to **Standard Cost**.

Configuring Costing Versions

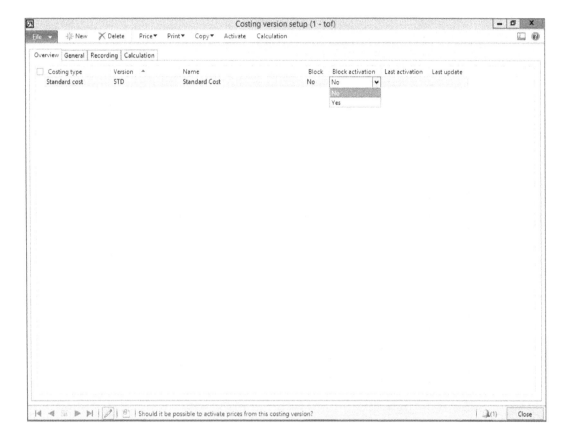

To finish off the step, click on the dropdown list for the **Block Activation** and set it to **No**. This allows you to activate the product cost against a product. If this is set to **Yes** then the cost will be purely for reference.

Configuring Costing Versions

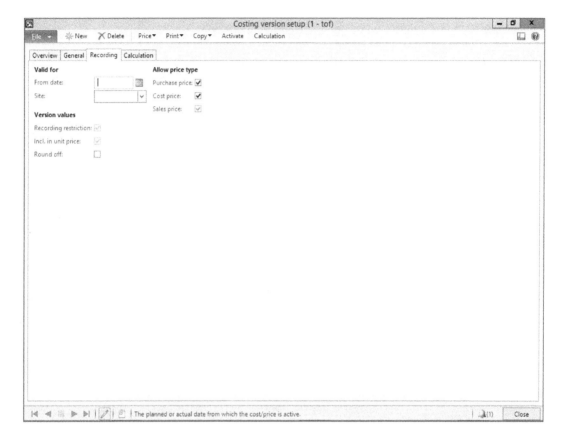

Now switch to the **Recording** tab, and we will make a few more tweaks.

Configuring Costing Versions

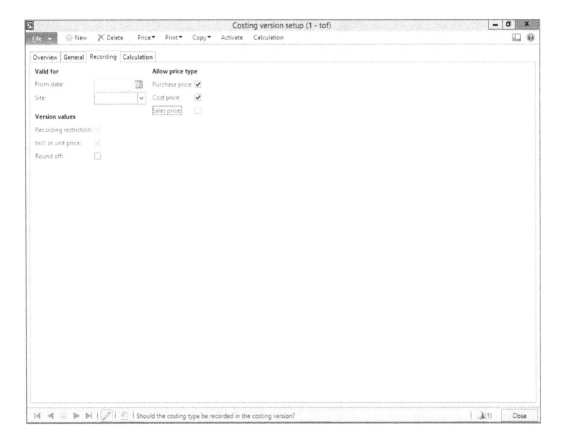

And all we will do is uncheck the **Sales Price** flag so that the system doesn't create a Sales Price Cost.

Configuring Costing Versions

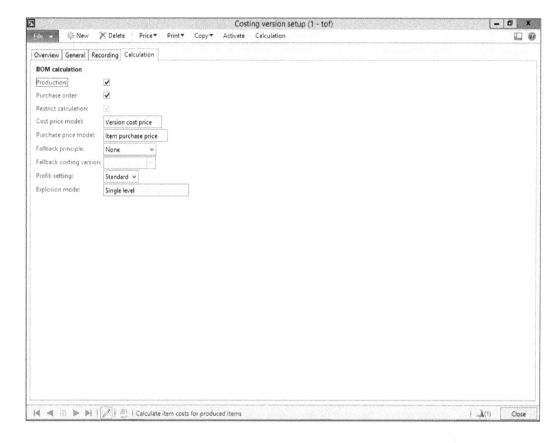

Finally, switch to the **Calculation** tab.

Configuring Costing Versions

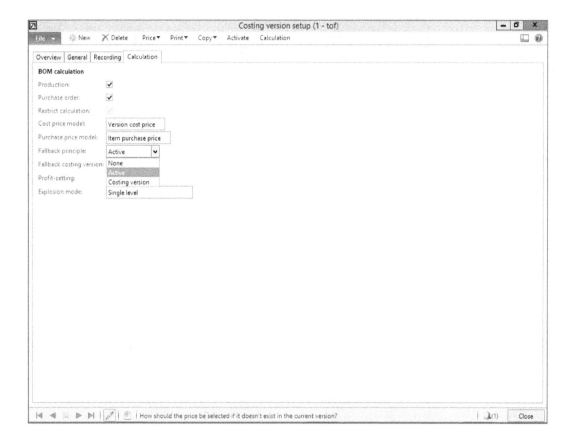

Click on the **Fallback Principle** dropdown list and change it from **None** to **Active** so that it will default to the active cost in a pinch.

Configuring Costing Versions

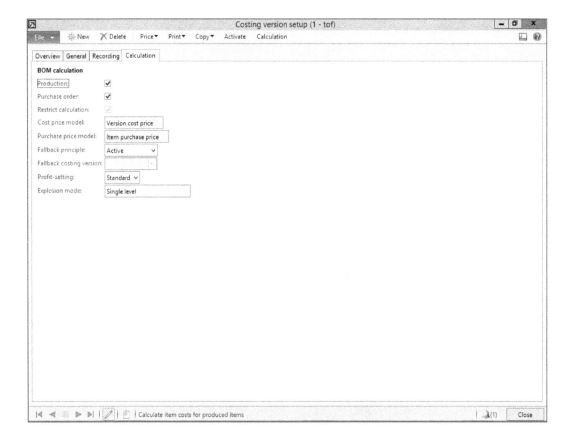

After you have done that you are finished on that **Costing Version**.

Configuring Costing Versions

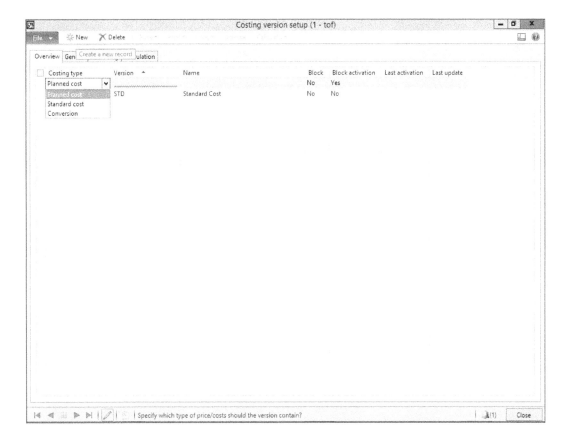

We will create one more **Costing Version** though, but this one will be just for planning purposes. So click on the **New** button in the menu bar to create a new record and select the **Planned Cost** value from the **Costing Type** dropdown list.

Configuring Costing Versions

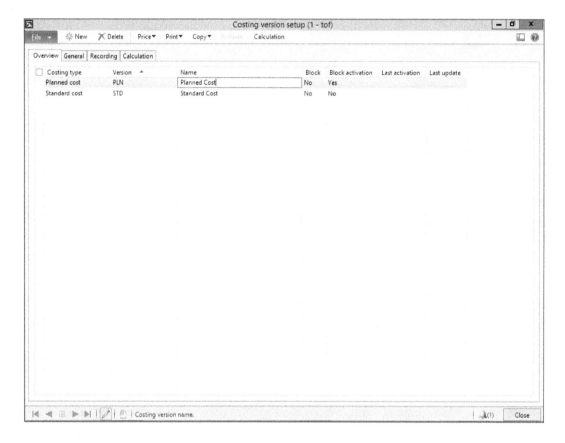

Set the **Version** code to **PLN** and the **Name** to **Planned Cost.**

Configuring Costing Versions

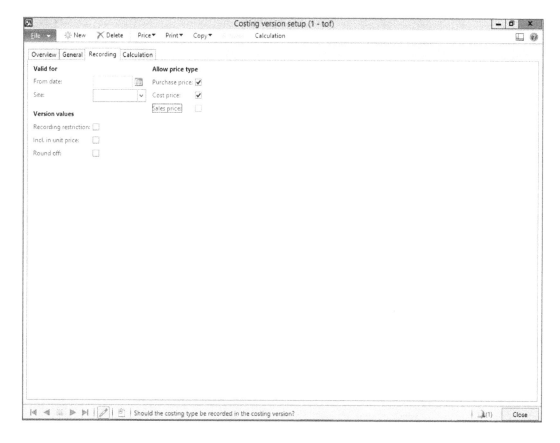

Switch to the **Recording** Tab and uncheck the **Sales Price** flag.

Configuring Costing Versions

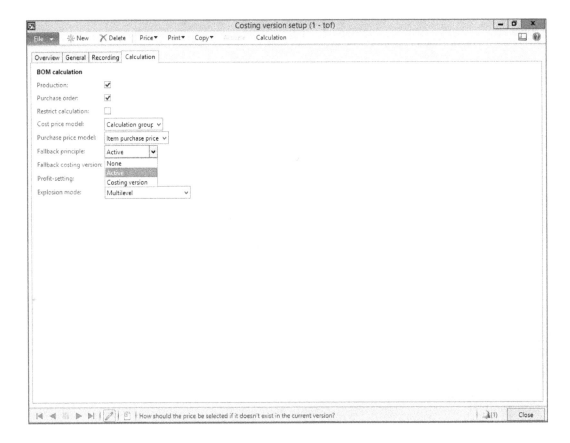

And then switch to the **Calculation** tab and set the **Fallback Costing Version** to **Active.**

Configuring Costing Versions

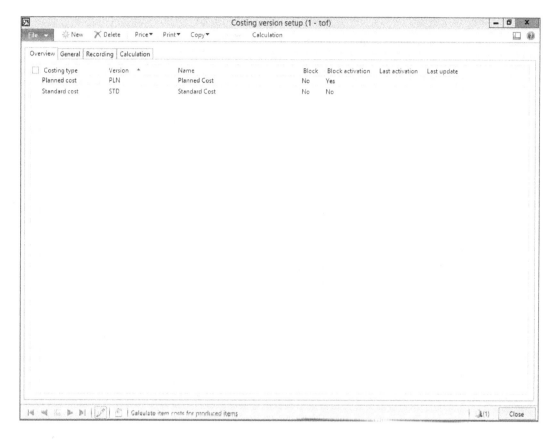

You can keep on adding additional **Costing Versions** if you like and when you are done, click on the **Close** button to exit from the form.

Configuring Calculation Groups

Next we will want to create a **Calculation Group**. These allow you to tweak how cost roll ups are performed and also what errors and warnings will be displayed. In this section we will just create a simple **Calculation Group** to get by.

Configuring Calculation Groups

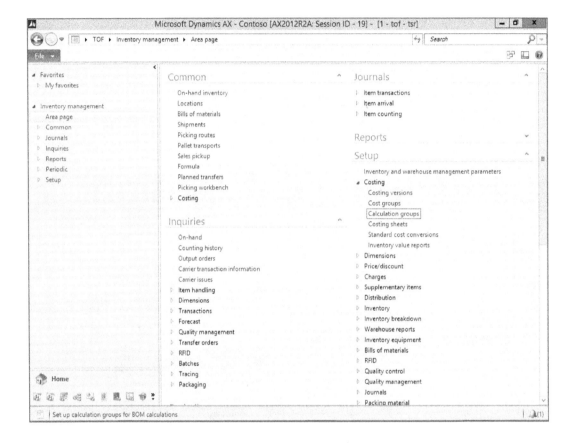

To do this, click on the **Calculation Groups** menu item within the **Costing** folder of the **Setup** group within the **Inventory Management** area page.

Configuring Calculation Groups

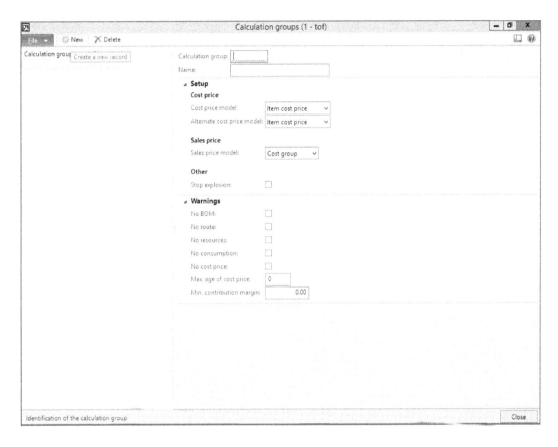

When the **Calculation Groups** maintenance form is displayed, click on the **New** button in the menu bar to create a new record.

Configuring Calculation Groups

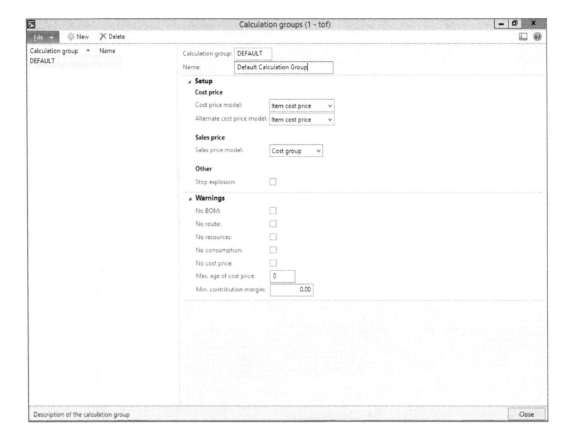

Set the **Calculation Group** code to **DEFAULT** and the **Name** to **Default Calculation Group**.

When you are done, just click on the **Close** button to exit from the form.

Configuring Inventory Journals

Next we will need to configure our **Inventory Journals** which are the movement journals that will tell the system what to do with the inventory, and will also allow you to differentiate between different transactions within the inventory movements. There are a few that we will need to set up, but don't worry this won't take much time.

Configuring Inventory Journals

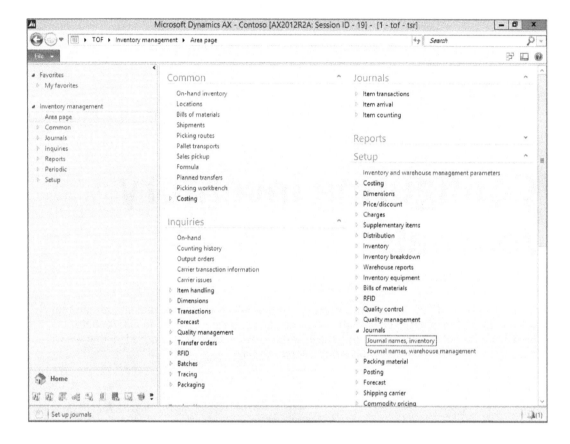

Start off by clicking on the **Journal Names, Inventory** menu item within the **Journals** folder of the **Setup** group within the **Inventory Management** area page.

Configuring Inventory Journals

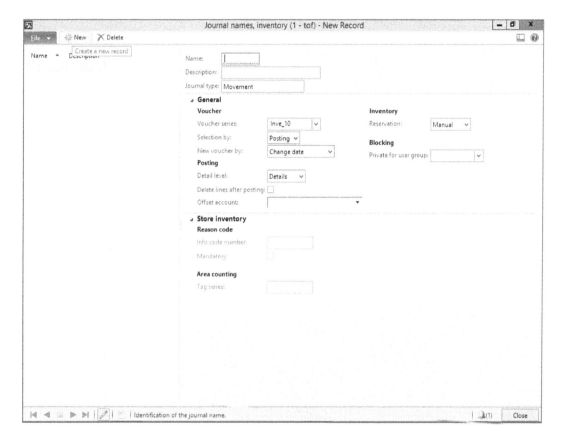

When the **Journal Names, Inventory** maintenance form is displayed, click on the **New** button in the menu bar to create a new record.

Configuring Inventory Journals

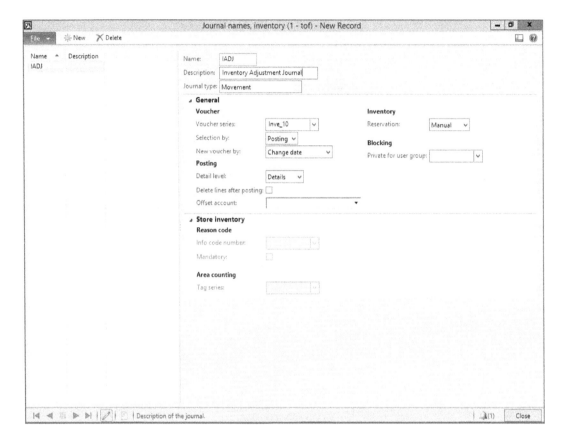

The first journal that we will create is for an Inventory adjustment so set the **Name** to **IADJ** and the **Description** to **Inventory Adjustment Journal**.

Configuring Inventory Journals

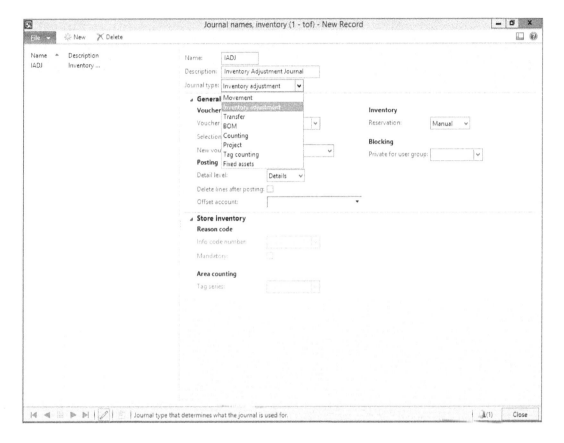

Then click on the **Journal Type** dropdown box and select the **Inventory Adjustment** item.

Configuring Inventory Journals

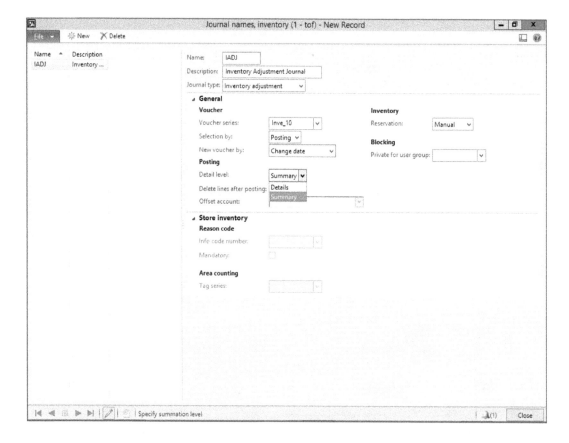

Then click on the **Detail Level** dropdown list within the **Posting** field group and select the **Summary** option to tell the system that you want to summarize the movements when you post them to the ledger so that you don't bloat out the journals.

Configuring Inventory Journals

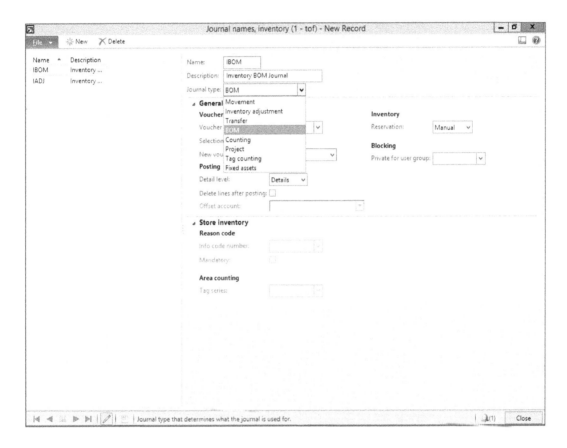

Next, we will create a BOM journal. Click on the **New** button in the menu bar to create a new record. Set the **Name** to **IBOM** and the **Description** to **Inventory BOM Journal**. Then click on the **Journal Type** dropdown list and select the **BOM** value.

Configuring Inventory Journals

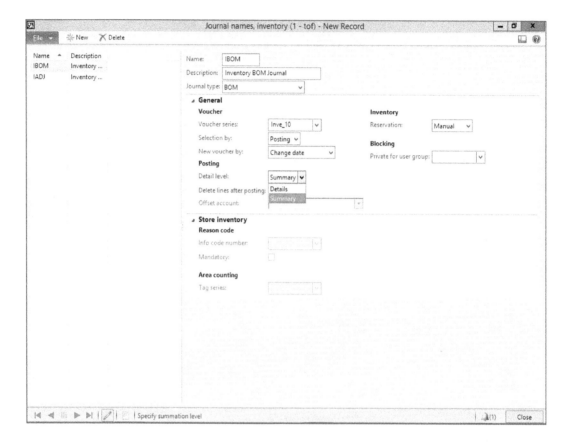

Then click on the **Detail Level** dropdown list within the **Posting** field group and select the
Summary option.

Configuring Inventory Journals

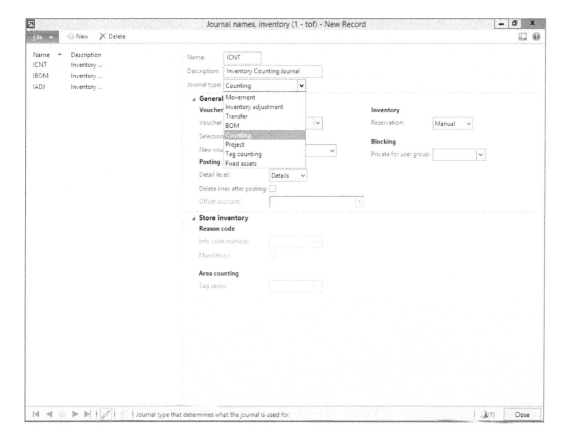

Next, we will create a counting journal type. So click on the **New** button in the menu bar to create a new record. Set the **Name** to **ICNT** and the **Description** to **Inventory Counting Journal**. Then click on the **Journal Type** dropdown list and select the **Counting** value.

Configuring Inventory Journals

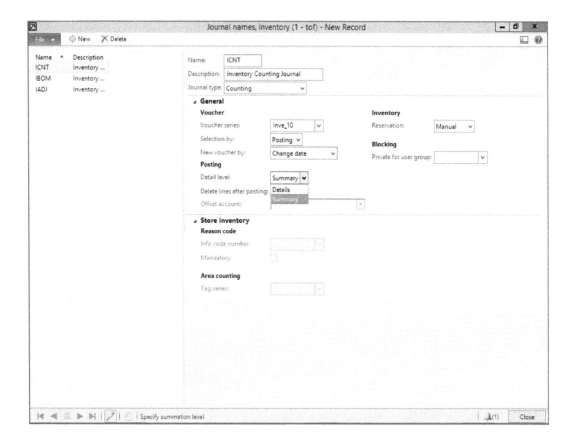

Then click on the **Detail Level** dropdown list within the **Posting** field group and select the **Summary** option.

Configuring Inventory Journals

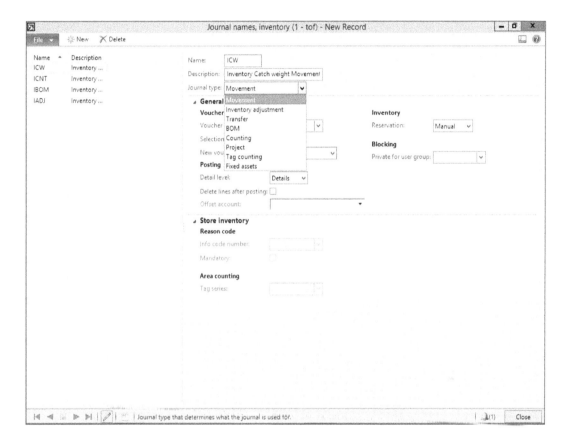

Now, we will create a couple of movement journals starting with a Catch Weight movement journal. Click on the **New** button in the menu bar to create a new record. Set the **Name** to **ICW** and the **Description** to **Inventory Catch Weight Movement**. Then click on the **Journal Type** dropdown list and select the **Movement** value.

© 2015 Blind Squirrel Publishing, LLC, All Rights Reserved
www.dynamicsaxcompanions.com

Configuring Inventory Journals

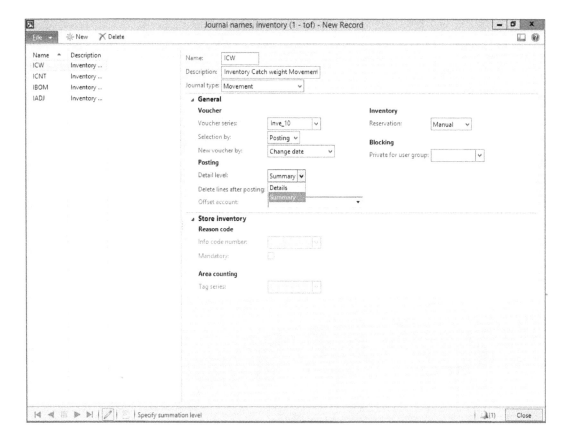

Then click on the **Detail Level** dropdown list within the **Posting** field group and select the
Summary option.

Configuring Inventory Journals

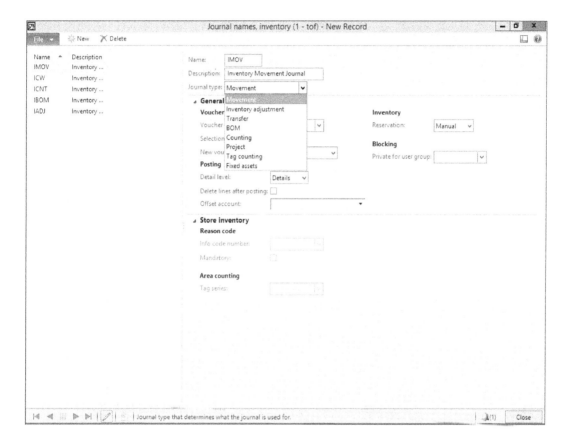

Then create a traditional movement journal by clicking on the **New** button in the menu bar to create a new record. Set the **Name** to **IMOV** and the **Description** to **Inventory Movement Journal**. Then click on the **Journal Type** dropdown list and select the **Movement** value.

Configuring Inventory Journals

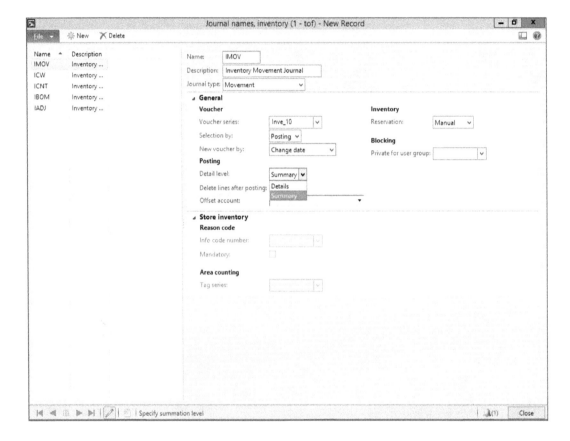

Then click on the **Detail Level** dropdown list within the **Posting** field group and select the **Summary** option.

Configuring Inventory Journals

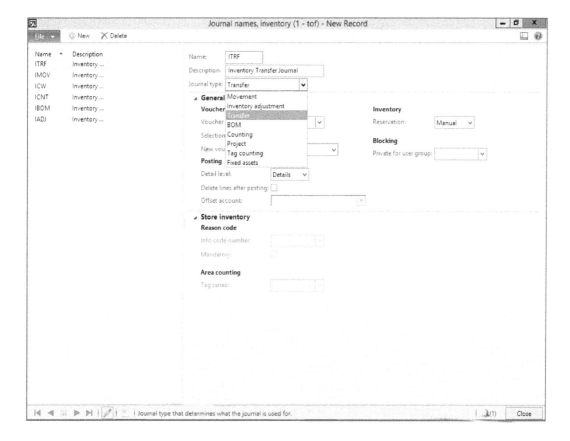

Now we will create a journal for inventory transfers. Click on the **New** button in the menu bar to create a new record. Set the **Name** to **ITRF** and the **Description** to **Inventory Transfer Journal**. Then click on the **Journal Type** dropdown list and select the **Transfer** value.

Configuring Inventory Journals

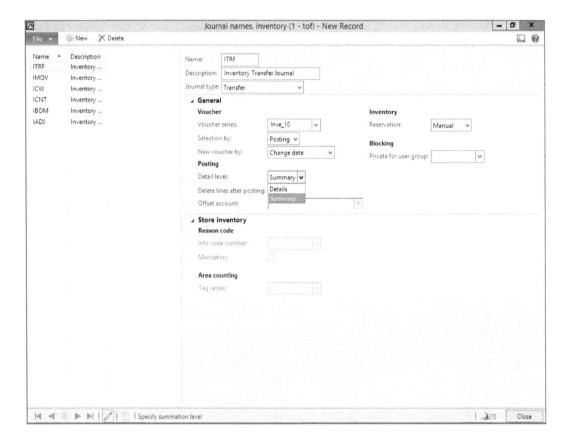

Then click on the **Detail Level** dropdown list within the **Posting** field group and select the **Summary** option.

Configuring Inventory Journals

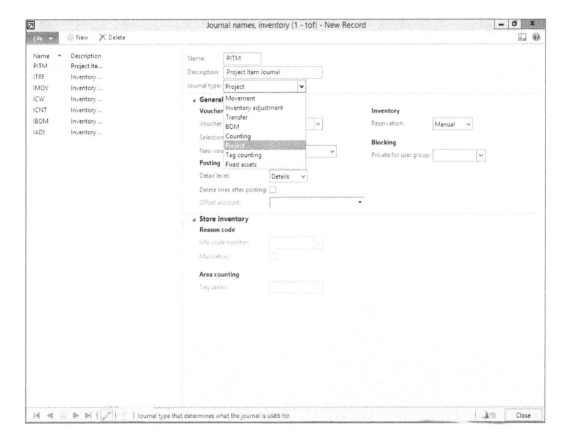

To prepare for much later on we will also create a few other journals starting with one for projects. Click on the **New** button in the menu bar to create a new record. Set the **Name** to **PITM** and the **Description** to **Project Item Journal**. Then click on the **Journal Type** dropdown list and select the **Project** value.

Configuring Inventory Journals

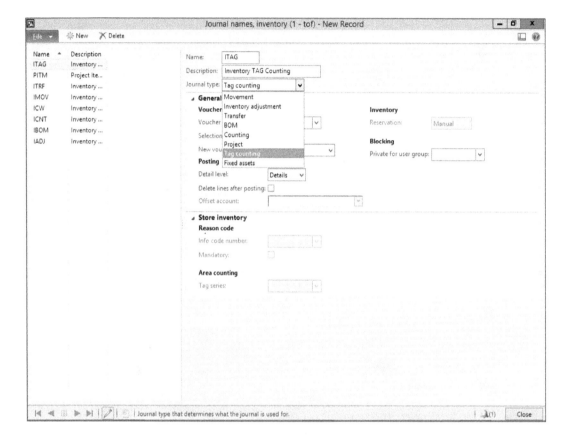

And finally we will create a journal for Tag Counting. Click on the **New** button in the menu bar to create a new record. Set the **Name** to **ITAG** and the **Description** to **Inventory Tag Counting**. Then click on the **Journal Type** dropdown list and select the **Tag Counting** value.

Configuring Inventory Journals

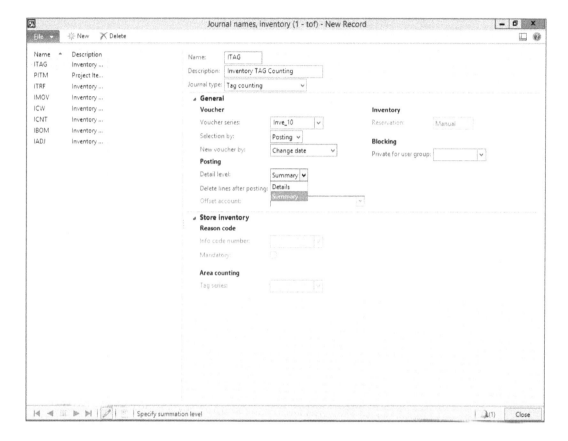

Then click on the **Detail Level** dropdown list within the **Posting** field group and select the **Summary** option.

After you have done that you can click on the **Close** button to exit out of the form.

Configuring The Inventory Management Parameters

Now that we have all of the codes and journals configured, there is just one last thing that we need to do before we move on and that its to set up some of the Inventory Management Parameters.

Configuring The Inventory Management Parameters

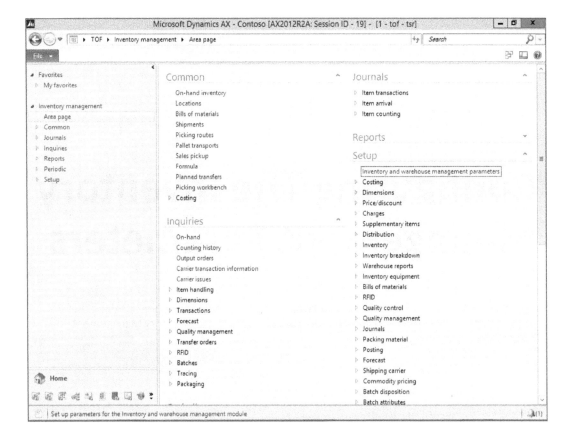

To do this, click on the **Inventory and Warehouse Management Parameters** menu item within the **Setup** group of the **Inventory Management** area page.

Configuring The Inventory Management Parameters

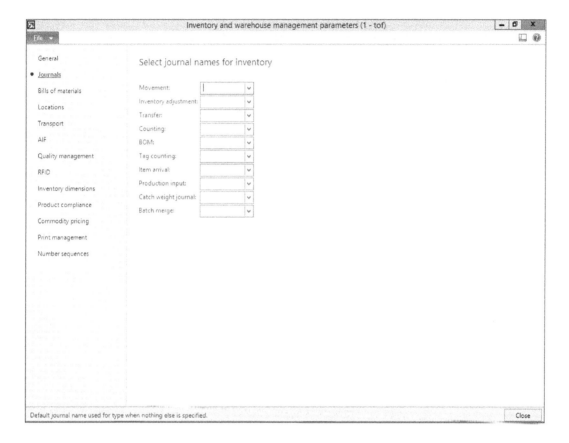

When the **Inventory and Warehouse Management Parameters** form is displayed, switch to the **Journals** page.

Configuring The Inventory Management Parameters

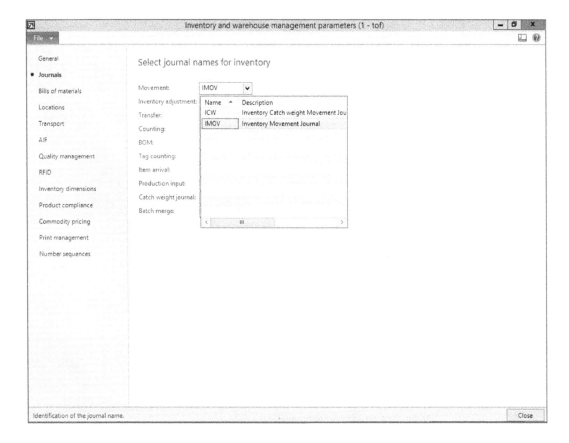

Click on the **Movement** dropdown list and select the **IMOV** journal code.

Configuring The Inventory Management Parameters

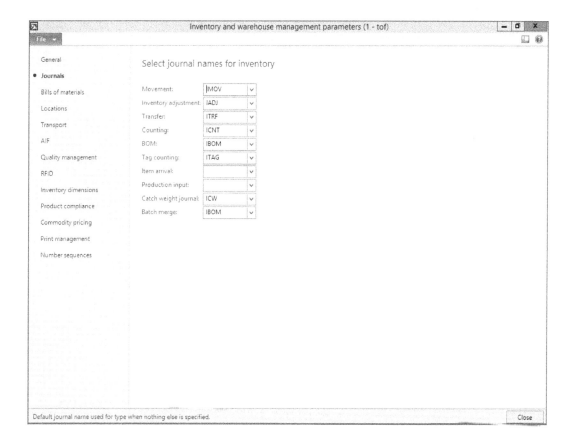

Keep on updating the Journal default names with the following values.

Inventory Adjustment	IADJ
Transfer	ITRF
Counting	ICNT
BOM	IBOM
Tag Counting	ITAG
Catch Weight Journal	ICW
Batch Merge	IBOM

Configuring The Inventory Management Parameters

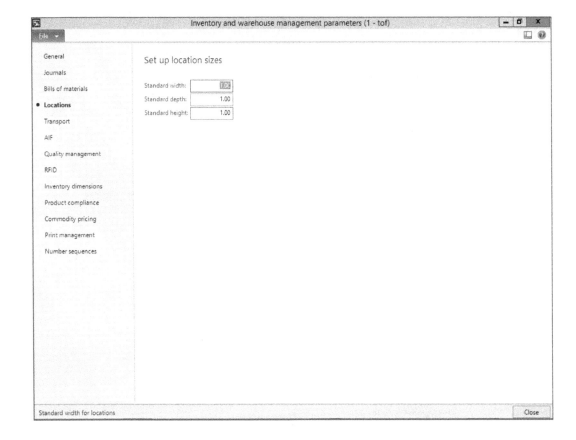

Next switch to the **Locations** page.

Configuring The Inventory Management Parameters

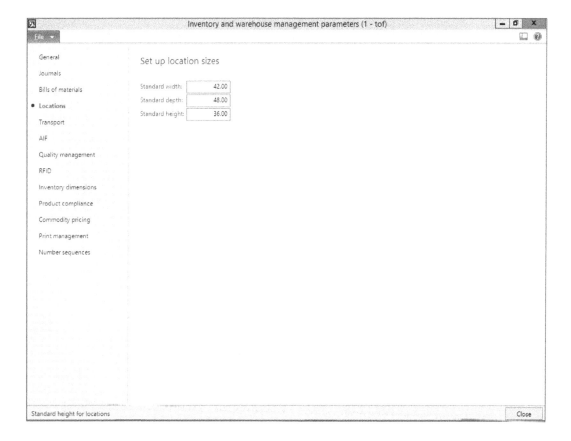

Here we can define the standard inventory location sizes which will default in later on and save us a lot of time. Set the **Standard Width** to **42** (inches), the **Standard Depth** to **48** (inches) and the **Standard Height** to **36** (inches).

Configuring The Inventory Management Parameters

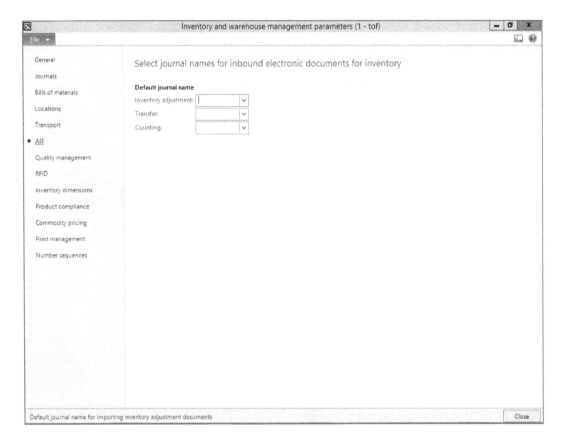

Now switch to the **AIF** page where we will define the default movement journals that we will use when called through an interface.

Configuring The Inventory Management Parameters

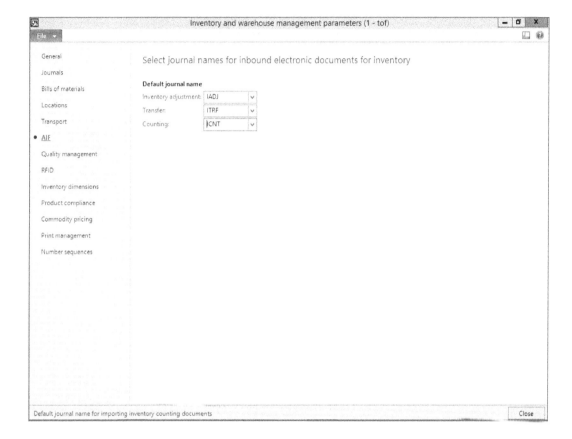

Set th Journal default names with the following values.

Inventory Adjustment	**IADJ**
Transfer	**ITRF**
Counting	**ICNT**

Configuring The Inventory Management Parameters

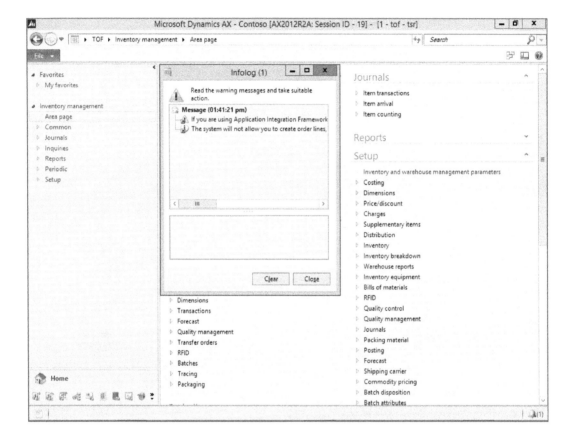

After you have finished that you can close the form. You will get a small warning mentioning that the AIF journals have been updated, and you can just close that and continue on.

CONFIGURING INVENTORY STRUCTURES

Now that we have the inventory management codes and controls configured we can start modelling our sites, warehouses, and inventory locations so that we can start tracking our inventory.

Creating New Sites

The first structure that we need to create is a **Site** which is a way that we can group common warehouses together. Sites also have other benefits because you can track different costs at the Site level as well.

Creating New Sites

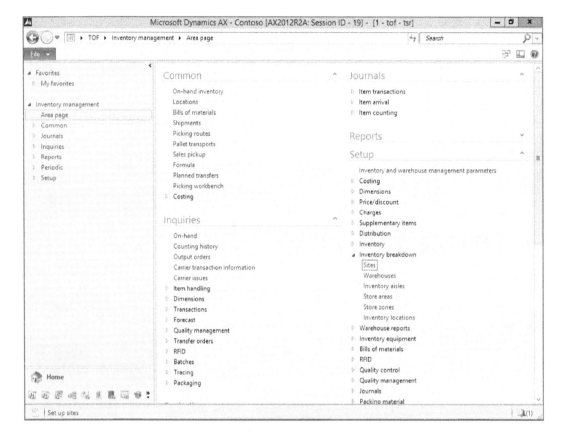

To do this, click on the **Sites** menu item within the **Inventory Breakdown** folder of the **Setup** group within the **Inventory Management** area page.

Creating New Sites

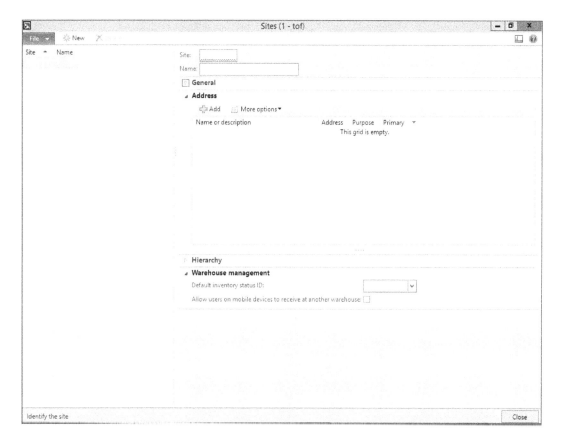

When the **Sites** maintenance form is displayed, click on the **New** button in the menu bar to create a new record.

Creating New Sites

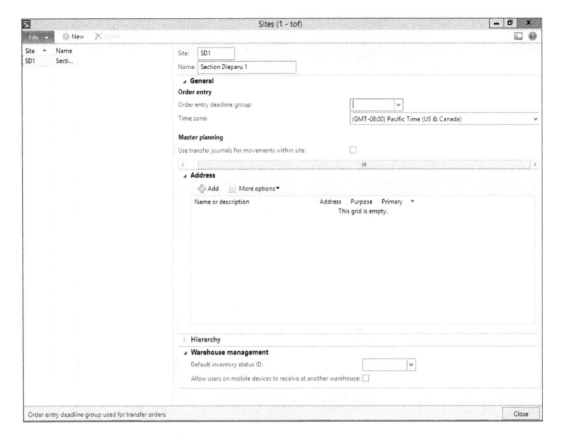

Set the **Site** code to **SD1** and the **Name** to **Section Dieparu 1**.

Creating New Sites

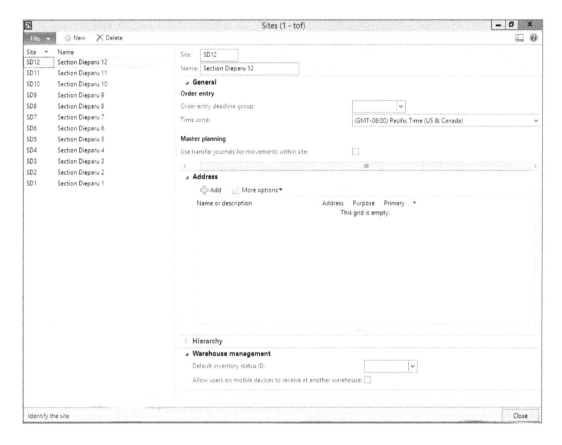

Repeat the process for all other sites that you want to manage within your organization and when you are done, click on the **Close** button to exit from the form.

Configuring Warehouses

Once you have configured your default sites, you can start building your warehouses.

Configuring Warehouses

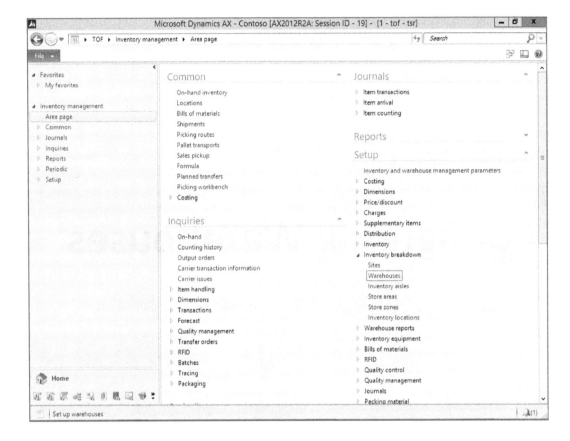

To do this, click on the **Warehouses** menu item within the **Inventory Breakdown** folder of the **Setup** group within the **Inventory Management** area page.

Configuring Warehouses

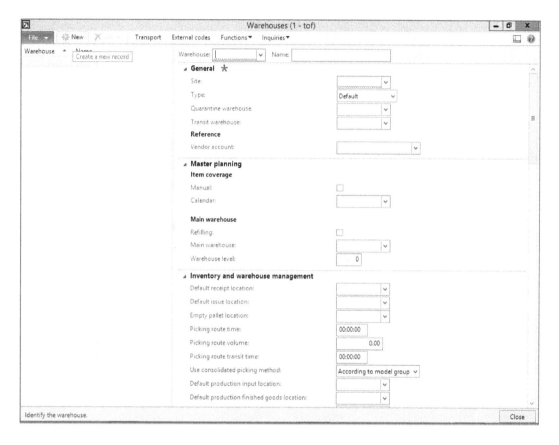

When the **Warehouses** maintenance form is displayed, click on the **New** button in the menu bar to create a new record.

Configuring Warehouses

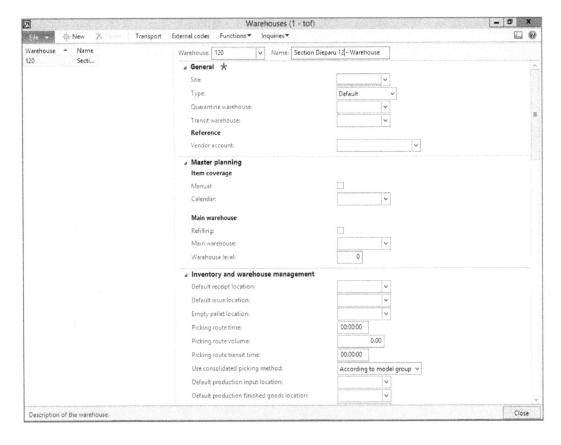

Set the **Warehouse** code to **120** and the **Name** to **Section Dieparu 12 – Warehouse**.

Configuring Warehouses

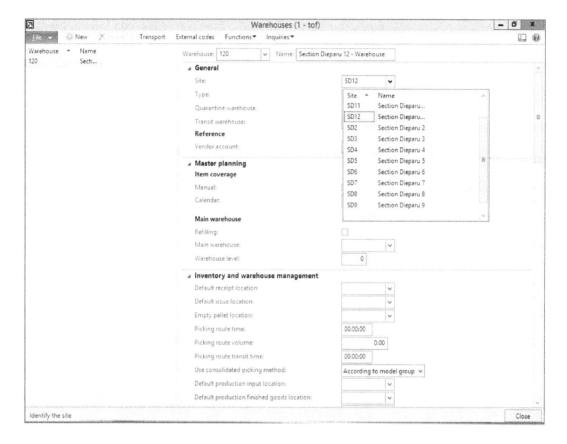

Then click on the **Site** dropdown list and select the **SD12** site.

Configuring The Default Inventory Location Structure

Once we have a warehouse we can start defining the inventory locations within the warehouse. The first step in doing this is to tell the warehouse how it's locations will be structured.

Configuring Warehouses

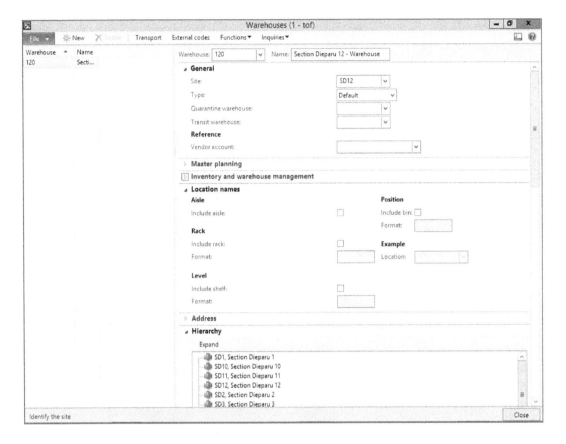

To do this start off by scrolling down to the **Location Names** tab group and expanding it.

This tab allows you to specify if your warehouse uses **Aisles**, **Racks**, **Levels** and also **Positions** within the location and also allows you to set default formats for the locations.

Configuring Warehouses

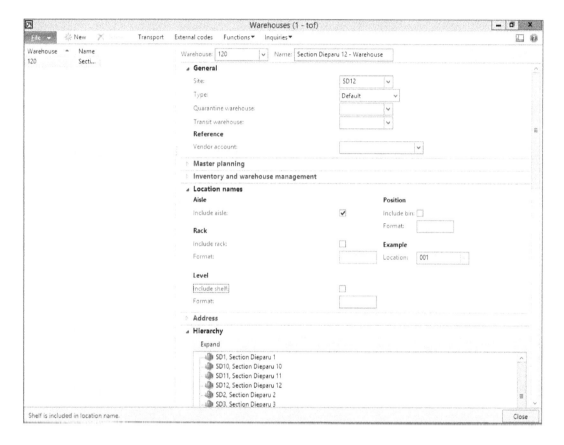

Start off by checking the **Include Aisle** flag.

Configuring Warehouses

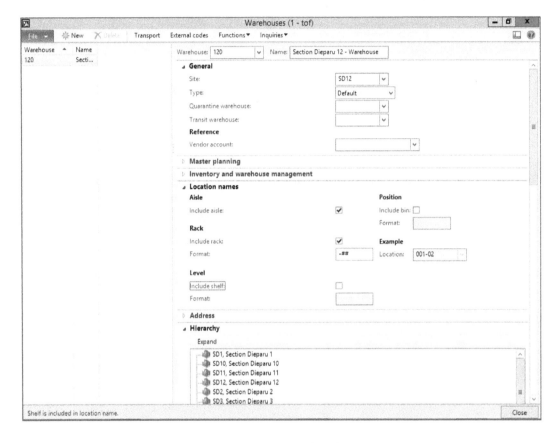

Then check the **Include Rack** flag and set the **Format** field for the rack to be **-##**. Notice that the **Example** field is starting to be populated with the default location code format.

Configuring Warehouses

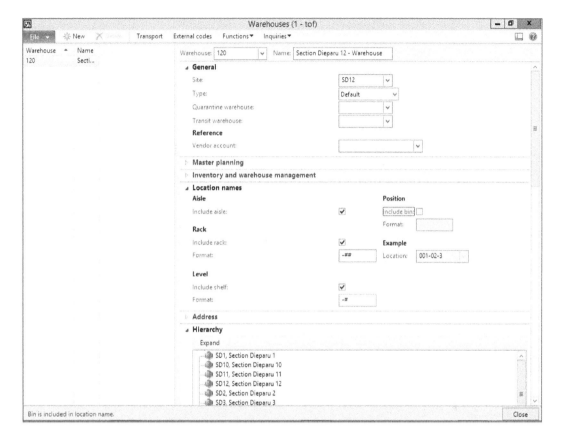

For our warehouse we will have multiple levels within each rack, so check the **Include Level** flag and set the **Format** to **-#**.

Using The Location Wizard To Create Your Locations

Now that we have the default location formats configured we start creating some inventory locations within our warehouse. You can do this manually, or you can take a shortcut and get the system to build the locations for you.

Configuring Warehouses

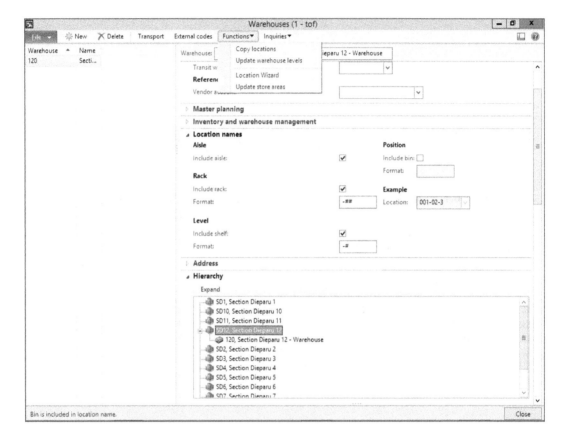

To do this, click on the **Functions** menu within the menu bar and select the **Location Wizard** menu item.

Configuring Warehouses

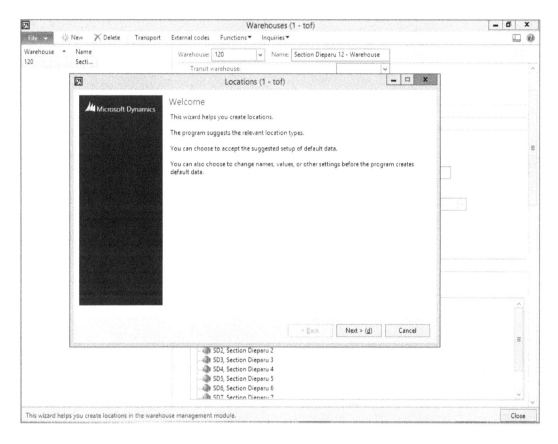

When the **Locations** wizard form is displayed, click on the **Next** button to skip past the welcome screen.

Configuring Warehouses

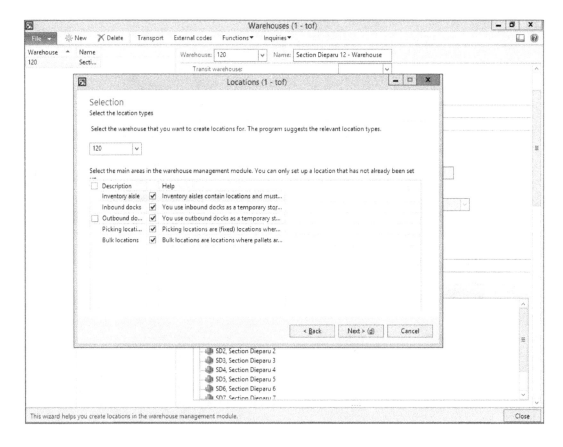

The next screen will show you all of the different locations that the wizard will create based off the location elements that you just chose. You can stop the system from creating particular locations if you like, although we will keep them all enabled and click the **Next** button.

Configuring Warehouses

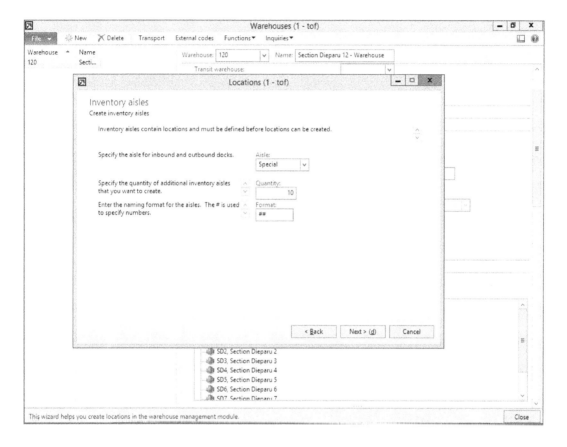

Next you will be asked for how many **Special** inventory locations you want to create,

Configuring Warehouses

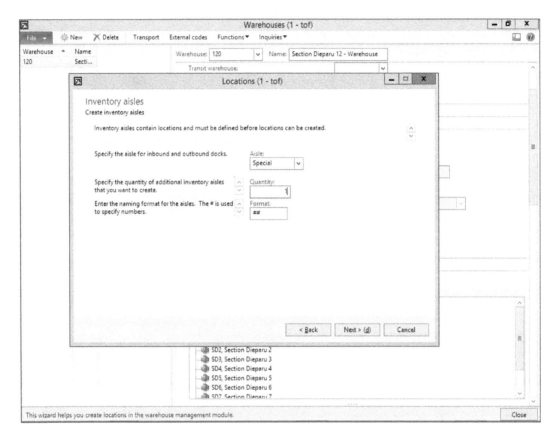

Change the **Quantity of Additional Aisles** from 10 to 1 to simplify the warehouse and then click the **Next** button.

Configuring Warehouses

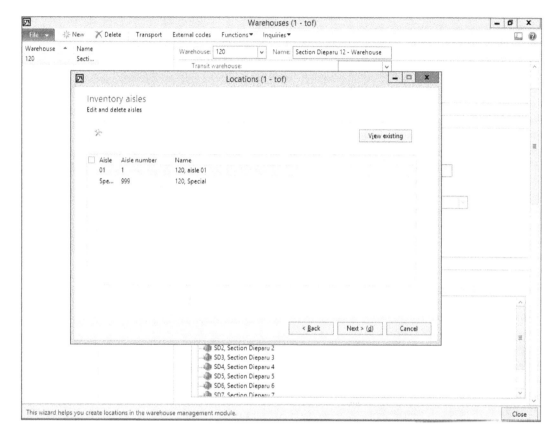

You will now see that the system is going to create two locations, and you can click the **Next** button to continue on.

Configuring Warehouses

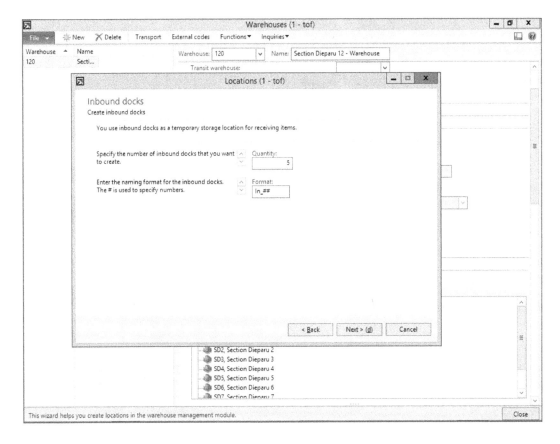

Next you will be asked how many **Inbound Docks** you have in the warehouse.

Configuring Warehouses

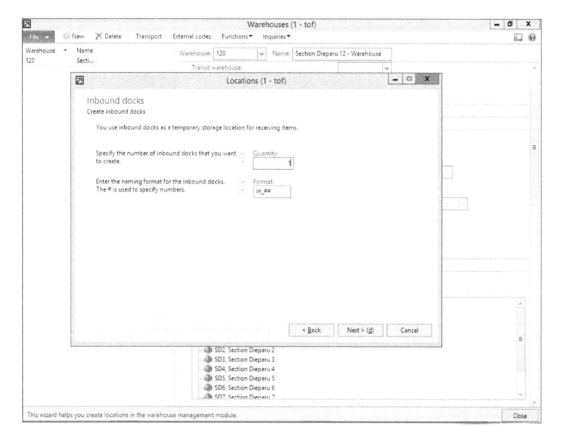

Change the number from **5** to **1** and then click on the **Next** button.

Configuring Warehouses

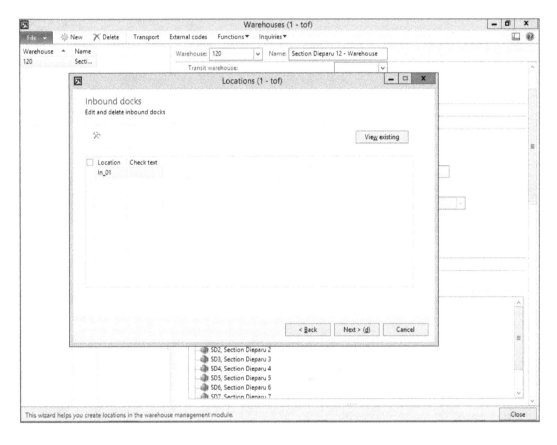

Again you will get confirmation that only one location is being created and you can click on the **Next** button to continue on.

Configuring Warehouses

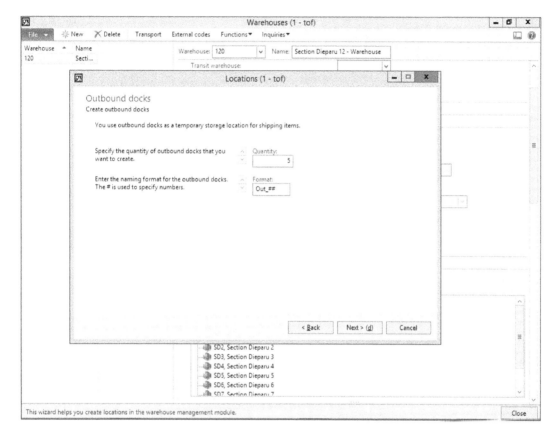

Now you will be asked to specify how many **Outbound Docks** you will have in the warehouse.

Configuring Warehouses

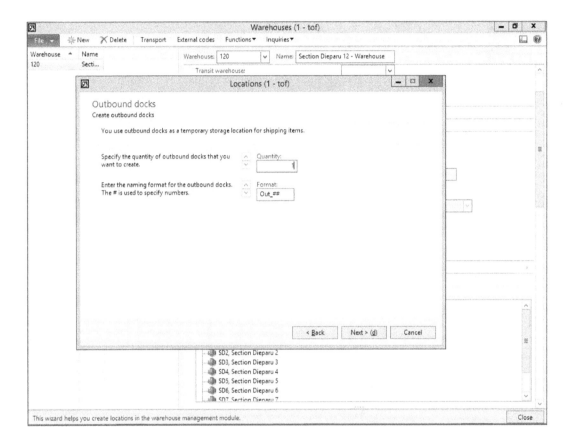

Change the number from **5** to **1**.

Configuring Warehouses

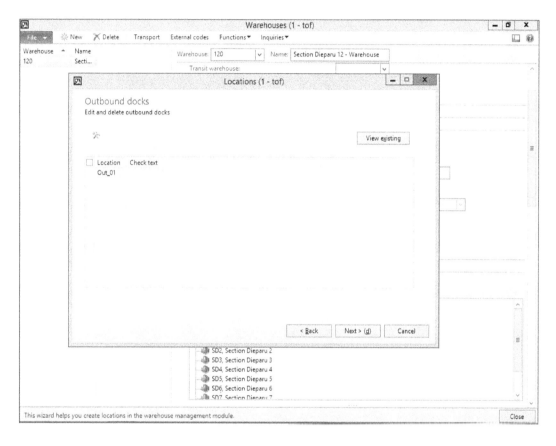

Then you will get confirmation that only one location is being created and you can click on the **Next** button to continue on.

Configuring Warehouses

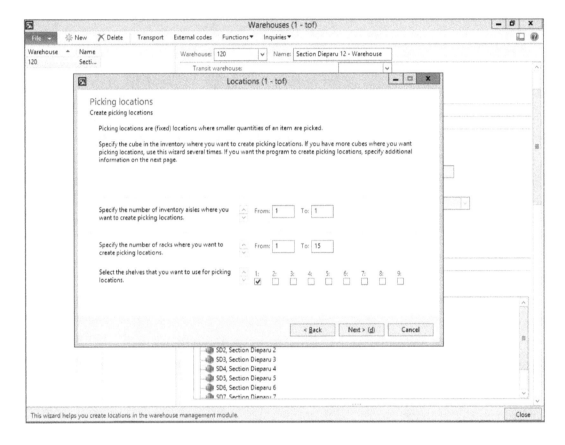

Next we need to specify how many **Picking Locations** we need to create. Here we can specify the number of aisles that we want to create, the number of racks that will be on each aisle, and also which shelves will be pickable.

Configuring Warehouses

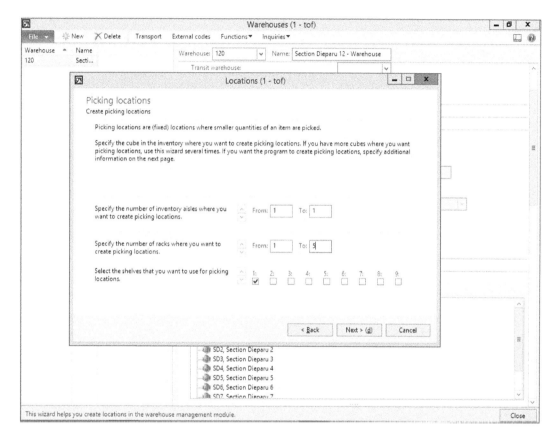

Change the maximum number of racks from **10** to **5** to make the warehouse a little smaller and then click on the **Next** button.

Configuring Warehouses

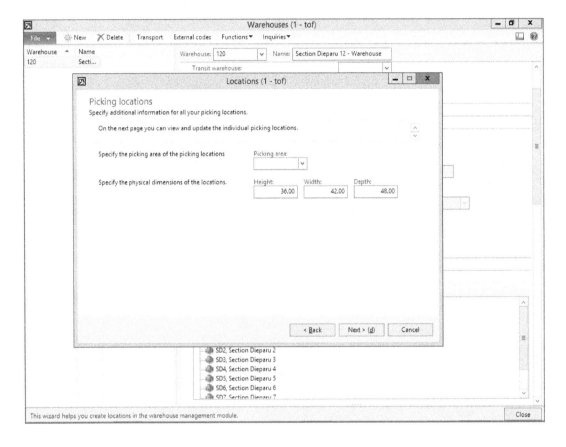

Next we will be asked for the physical dimensions for the picking locations. Since we set these up already within the parameters, the dimensions will default in for us. If you want you can change the default dimensions, and then click on the **Next** button to continue on.

Configuring Warehouses

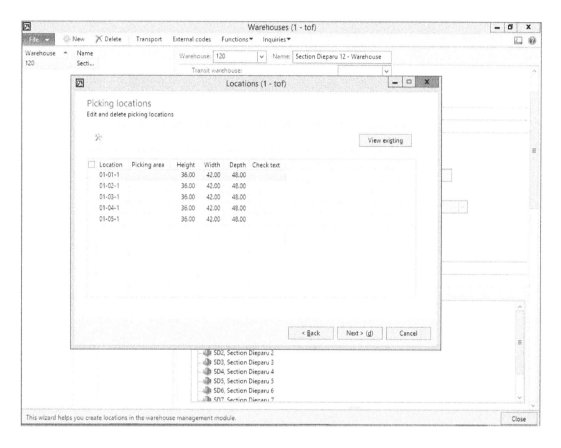

Now you will see the five locations that are being creates, and you can click on the **Next** button to continue on.

Configuring Warehouses

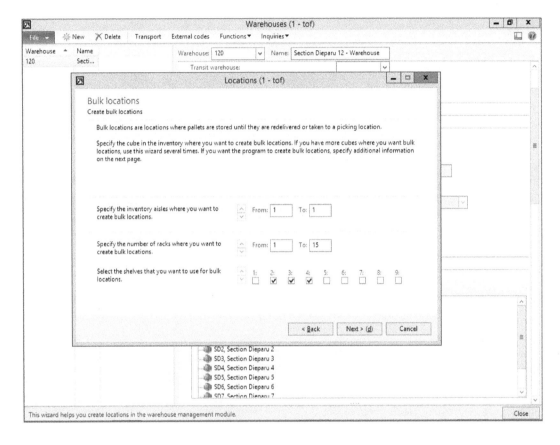

Now we need to repeat the same process for the bulk locations.

Configuring Warehouses

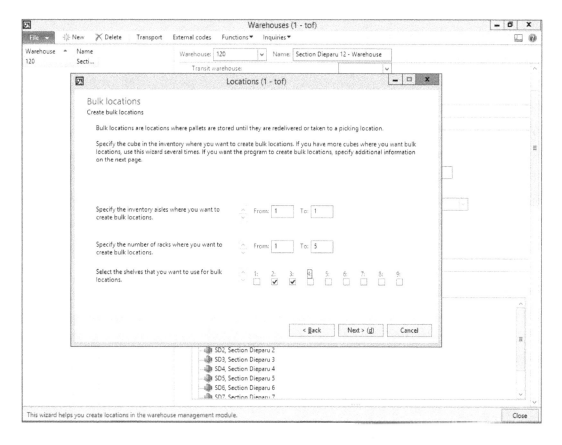

Change the maximum number of racks from **10** to **5** to match the picking locations, and then uncheck the **4** flag on the levels. This will tell the system that we just have two bulk location levels.

Note: Be careful not to overlap the picking and the bulk location levels. Dynamics AX will complain about duplicates if you do.

When you are done, click on the **Next** button to continue on.

Configuring Warehouses

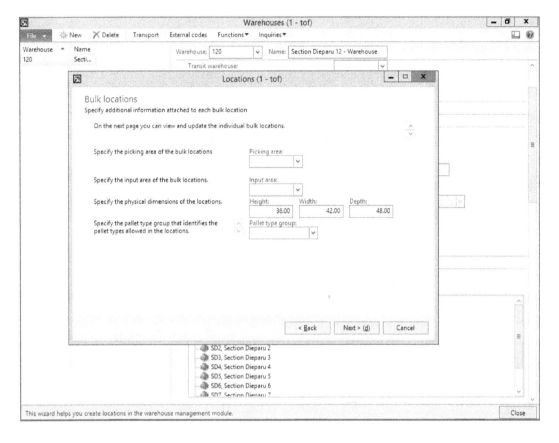

We will be asked again for the physical dimensions for the bulk locations. If you want you can change the default dimensions, and then click on the **Next** button to continue on.

Configuring Warehouses

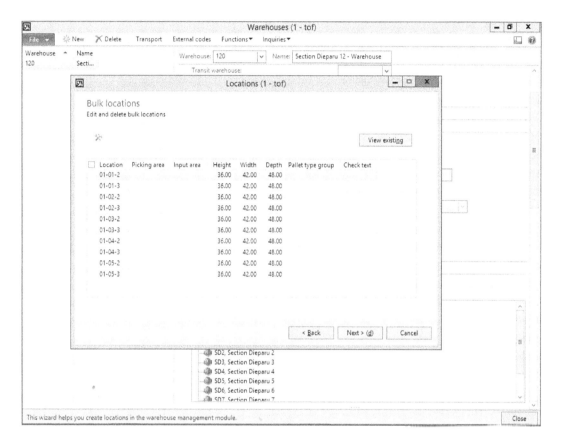

Now you will see the extra ten locations that are being created and you can click the **Next** button to continue on.

Configuring Warehouses

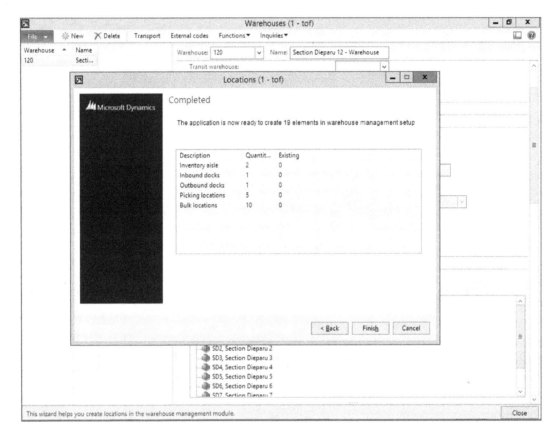

Finally you will get a summary of all the locations that are being created. If it all looks good then you can click on the **Finish** button to start the wizard processing.

Updating The Warehouses Default Locations

There is one last step within the warehouse setup that we need to do, and that is to define the default locations that will be used within the warehouse.

Updating The Warehouses Default Locations

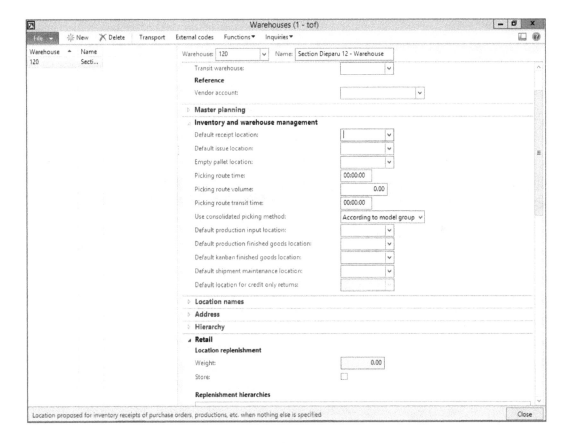

To do this, return back to the **Warehouses** form and expand out the **Inventory and Warehouse Management** tab.

Updating The Warehouses Default Locations

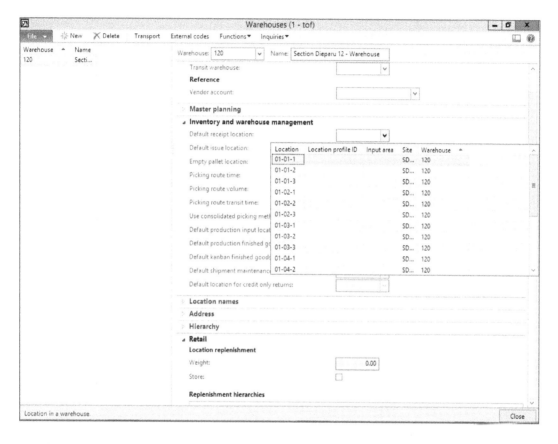

Click on the dropdown list for the **Default Receipt Location** and you will see all of the locations that you just created. Select the **01-01-1** location.

Updating The Warehouses Default Locations

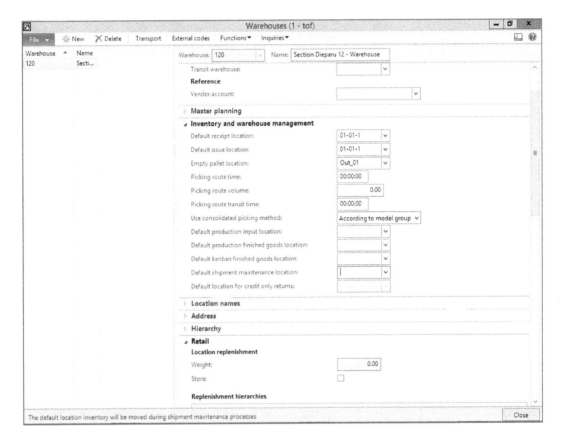

Click on the **Default Issue Location** dropdown list and select the **01-01-1** location, and then click on the **Empty Pallet Location** dropdown list and set that to the **Out_01** location for easy pickup.

Once you have done that you can just click on the **Close** button and exit from the form.

Creating Quarantine Warehouses

In addition to being able to create normal warehouses, there are also special warehouses that you can set up to track the movement of inventory. The first is a **Quarantine** warehouse.

Creating Quarantine Warehouses

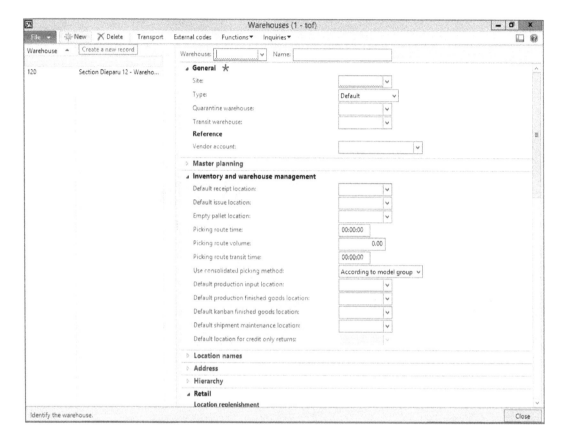

To set a **Quarantine** warehouse up, open up the **Warehouses** maintenance form and click on the **New** button in the menu bar to create a new record.

Creating Quarantine Warehouses

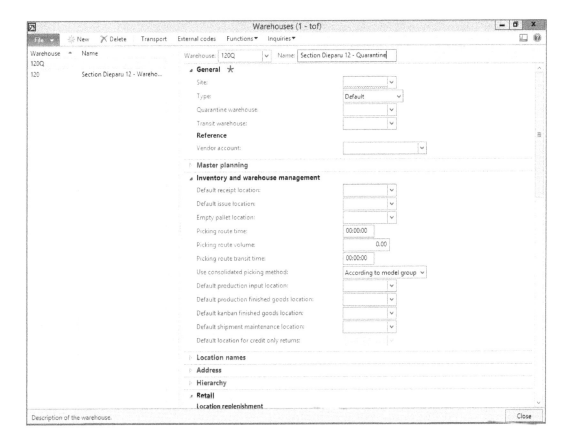

Set the **Warehouse** to **120Q** and the **Name** to **Section Dieparu 12 – Quarantine**.

Creating Quarantine Warehouses

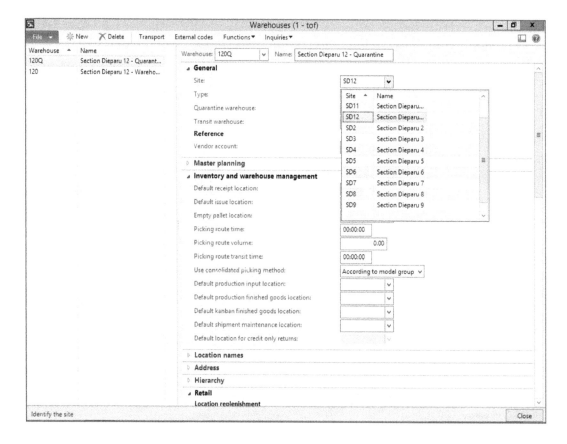

Then set the **Site** to **SD12**.

Creating Quarantine Warehouses

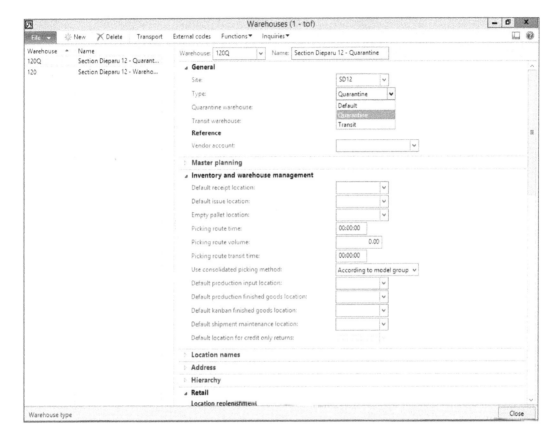

Now click on the **Type** dropdown list and select the **Quarantine** option to indicate that this is a quarantine warehouse.

Creating Quarantine Warehouses

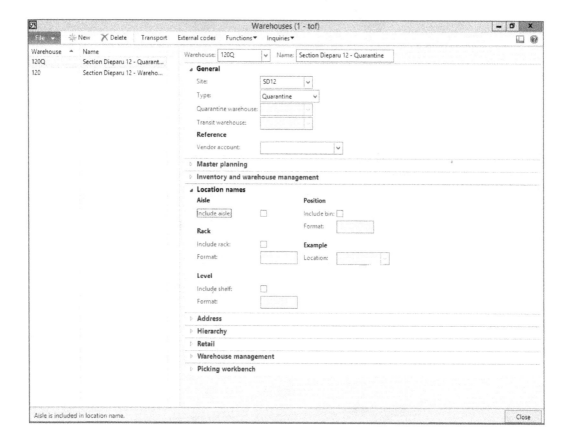

Next expand out the **Location Names** tab group.

Creating Quarantine Warehouses

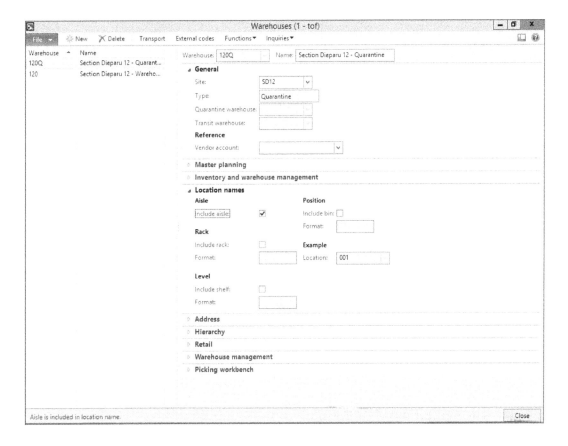

For this warehouse we don't need to track all of the racks and levels, so just check the **Include Aisle** flag.

Creating Quarantine Warehouses

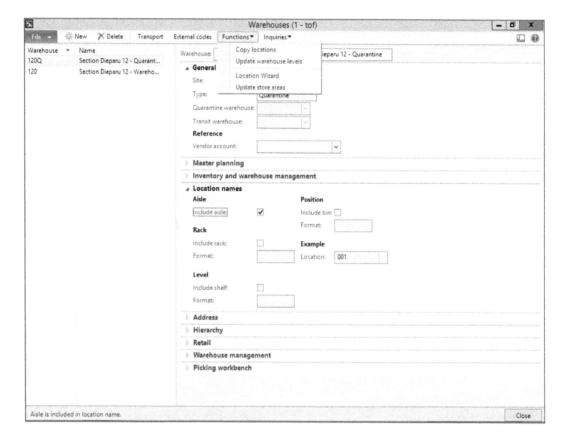

Then click on the **Functions** button in the menu bar and select the **Location Wizard** menu item.

Creating Quarantine Warehouses

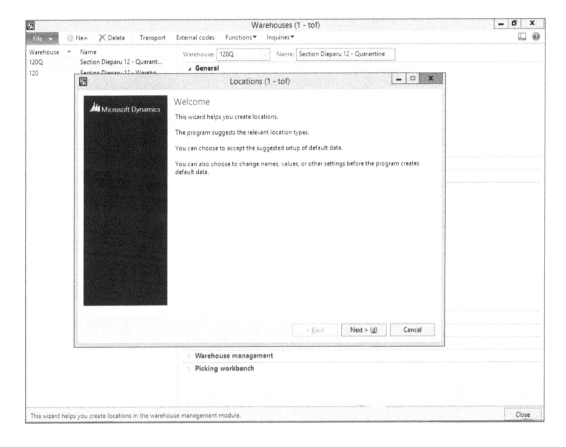

When the **Locations Wizard** is displayed, click on the **Next** button to start the setup.

Creating Quarantine Warehouses

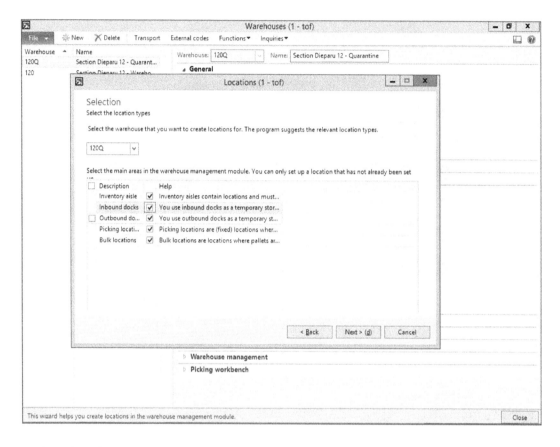

When the **Selection** page is displayed it defaults in to create all of the different location types.

Creating Quarantine Warehouses

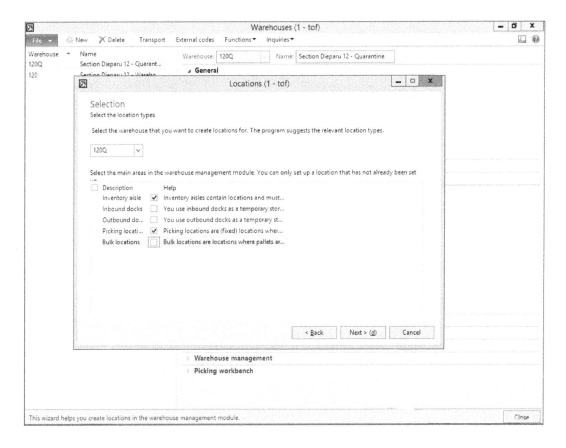

For this warehouse, we want to simplify it a little, so uncheck the **Inbound Docks**, the **Outbound Docks**, and the **Bulk Locations** and then click on the **Next** button.

Creating Quarantine Warehouses

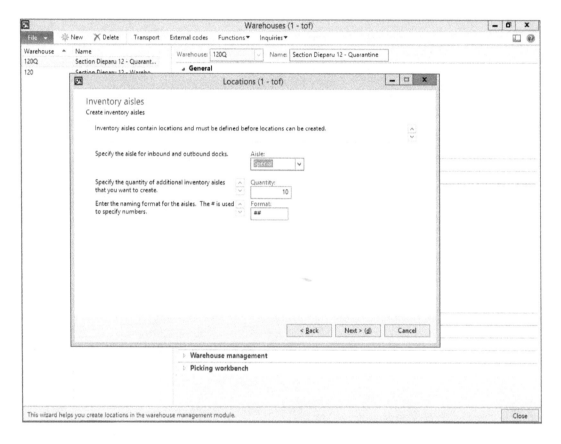

Next you will be asked for the number of inventory Aisles.

Creating Quarantine Warehouses

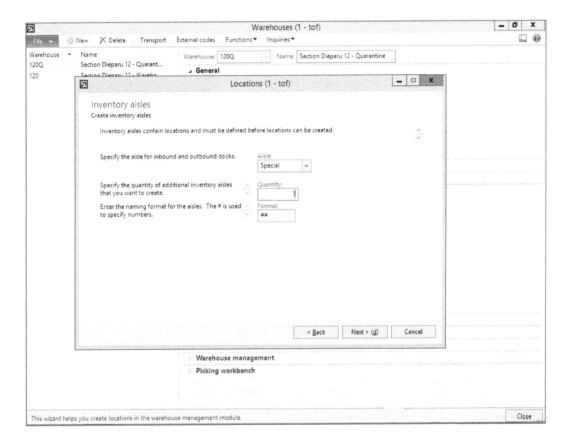

Change the number from **10** to **1** and then click on the **Next** button.

Creating Quarantine Warehouses

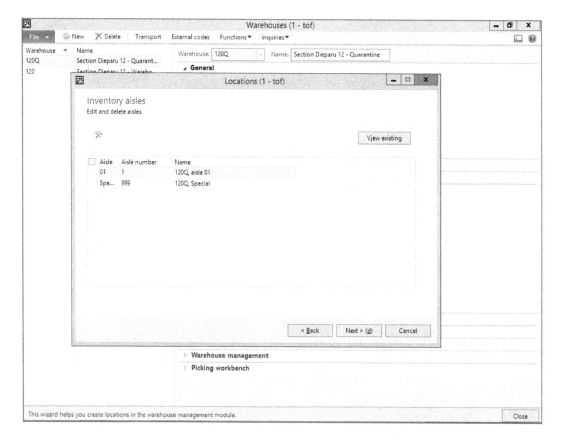

When the inventory aisles confirmation is displayed click on the **Next** button.

Creating Quarantine Warehouses

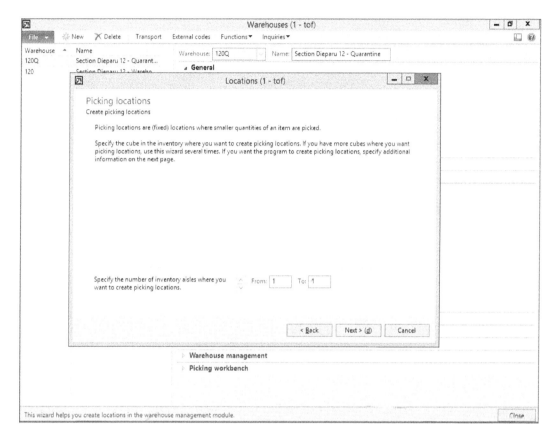

When the **Picking Locations** are displayed, just click on the **Next** button.

Creating Quarantine Warehouses

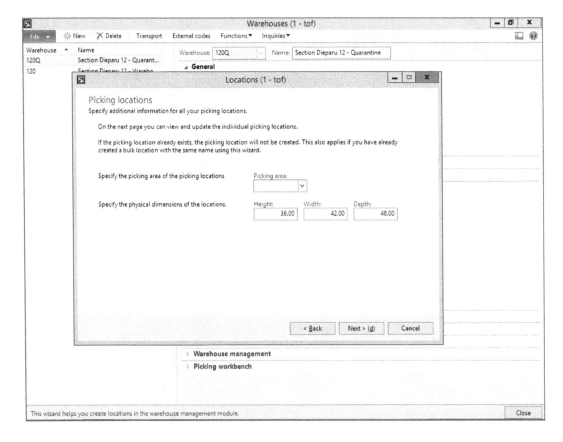

If you want you can adjust the size of the picking location, but for now we will just continue on and click on the **Next** button.

Creating Quarantine Warehouses

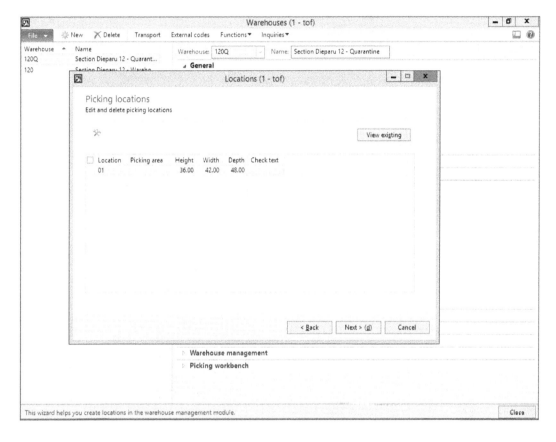

Next we will see the one location that is going to be created and you can click the **Next** button to continue on.

Creating Quarantine Warehouses

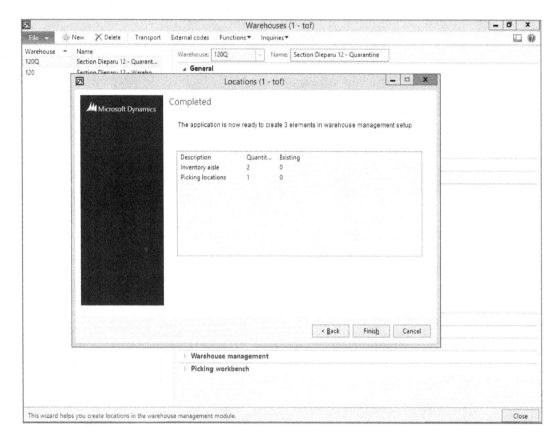

Now all that is left is to click on the **Finish** button and create the locations.

Creating Quarantine Warehouses

When you return back to the warehouses, expand out the **Inventory And Warehouse Management** tab so that you can see the default locations.

Creating Quarantine Warehouses

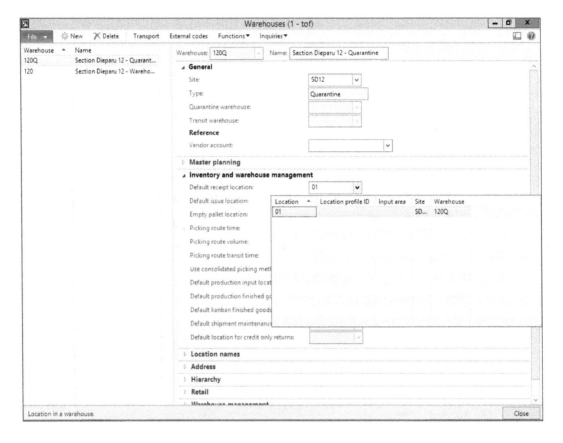

When you click on the **Default Receipt Location** dropdown you will be able to select the one location that was created.

Creating Quarantine Warehouses

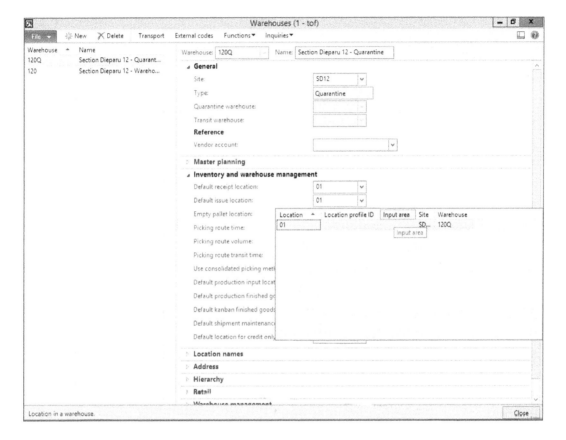

You can do the same again for the **Default Issue Location**.

Creating Quarantine Warehouses

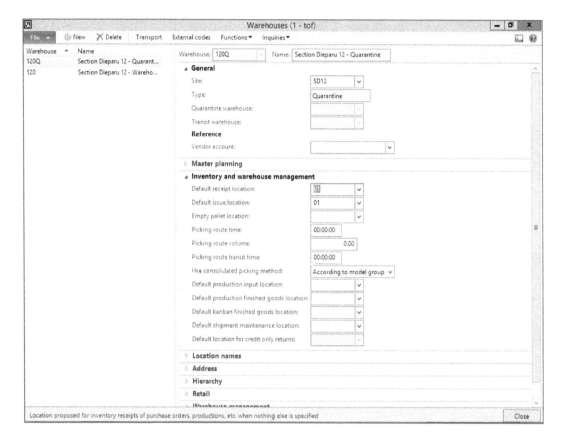

Now you have a quarantine warehouse.

Creating In Transit Warehouses

Another type of warehouse that you may want to create is an **In Transit** warehouse. This will allow you to track inventory that is being transferred to the warehouse but not yet received.

Creating In Transit Warehouses

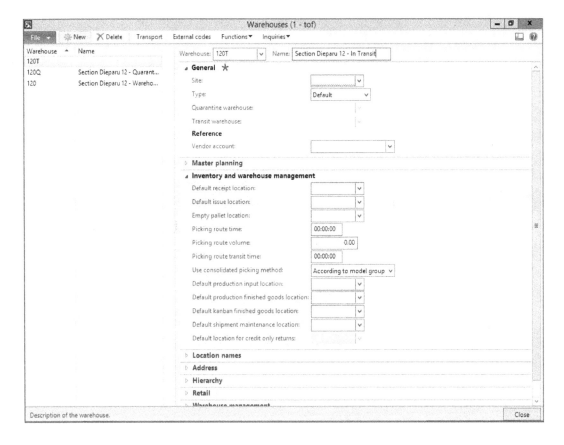

To do this, click on the **New** button in the menu bar to create a new record and set the **Warehouse** to **120T** and the **Name** to **Section Dieparu 12 – In Transit**.

174

Creating In Transit Warehouses

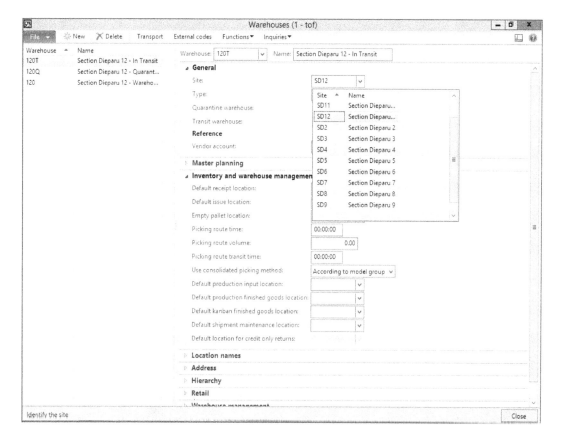

Click on the **Site** dropdown list and select the **SD12** site.

Creating In Transit Warehouses

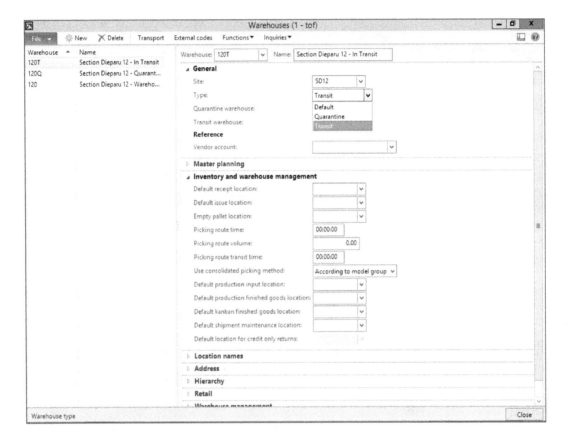

Then click on the **Type** dropdown list and select the **Transit** option.

Creating In Transit Warehouses

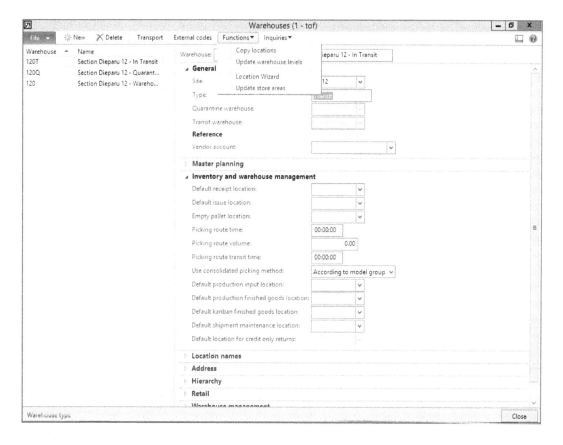

The transit warehouse will be a simple warehouse just like the quarantine one with only one location, so we can take a shortcut with the warehouse location setup and just copy the locations from the existing warehouse. To do this, click on the **Functions** menu item and select the **Copy Locations** menu item.

Creating In Transit Warehouses

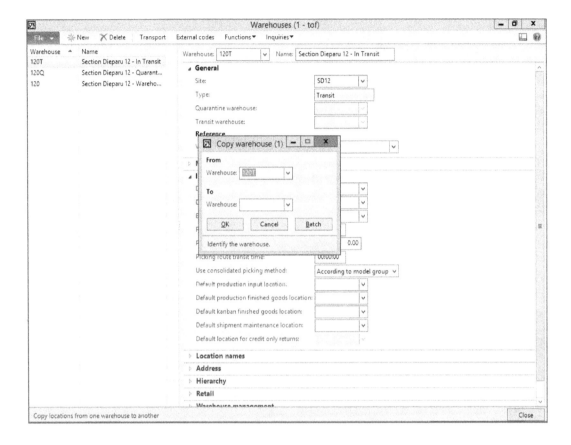

This will open up a **Copy Warehouse** dialog box.

Creating In Transit Warehouses

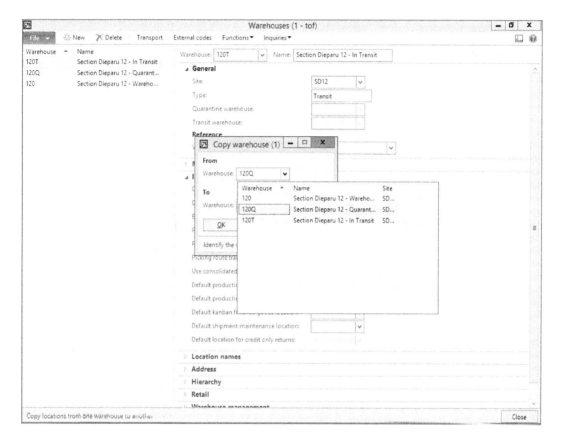

Click on the **From Warehouse** dropdown list and select the **120Q** warehouse.

Creating In Transit Warehouses

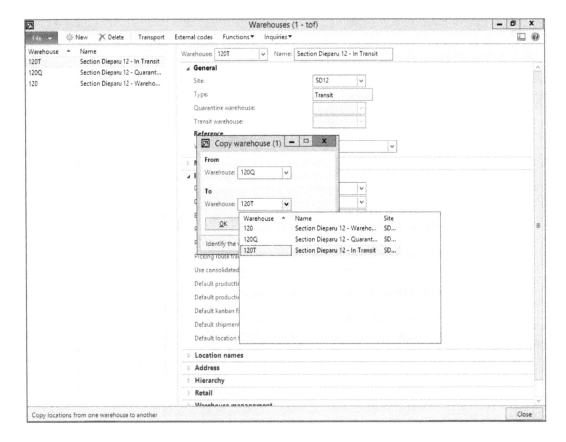

Then click on the **To Warehouse** and select the **120T** warehouse.

Creating In Transit Warehouses

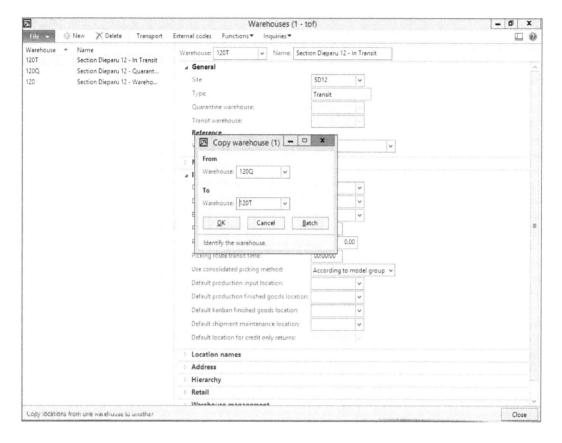

Then just click on the **OK** button to copy the locations.

Creating In Transit Warehouses

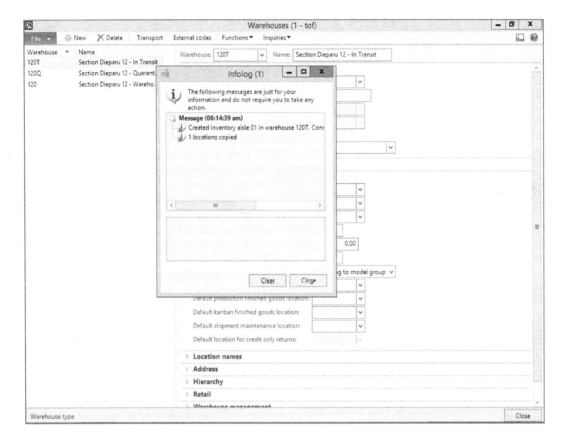

If everything works out then you will get an InfoLog that says that the warehouse has been copied.

Creating In Transit Warehouses

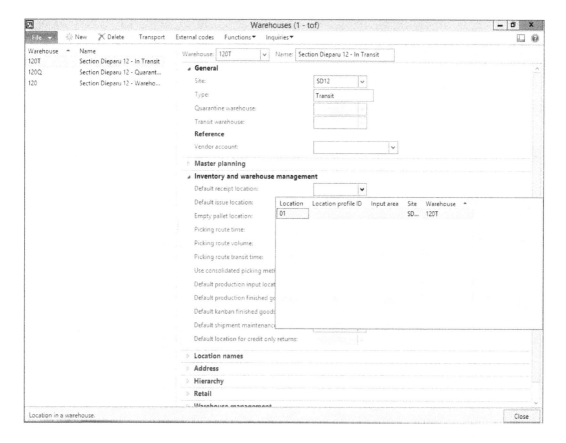

Now when you return back to the warehouse you will be able to click on the **Default Receipt Location** and you will have a location to select.

Creating In Transit Warehouses

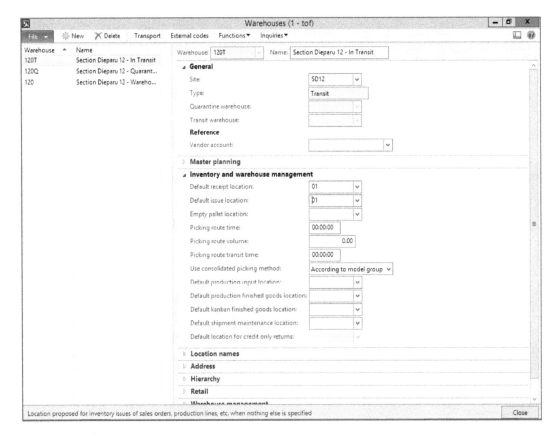

To finish off the warehouse, just click on the **Default Issue Location** and select the location that you want to use for that as well.

Assigning In Transit and Quarantine Warehouses To Existing Warehouses

Once you have created your Quarantine and In Transit warehouses, there is one final step that is required and that is just to link them to the existing warehouse so that it will use them.

Assigning In Transit and Quarantine Warehouses To Existing Warehouses

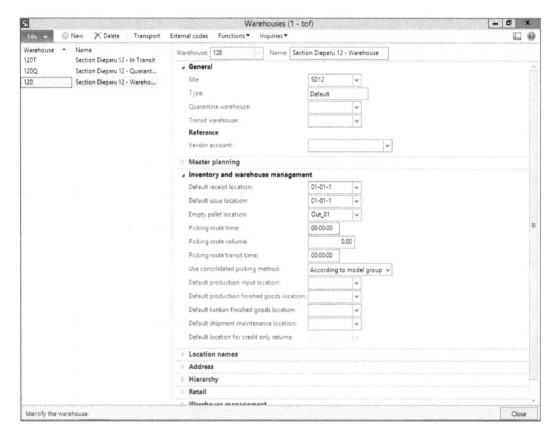

To do this, open up the Warehouses maintenance form and select the primary warehouse – in this example it's **120**.

Assigning In Transit and Quarantine Warehouses To Existing Warehouses

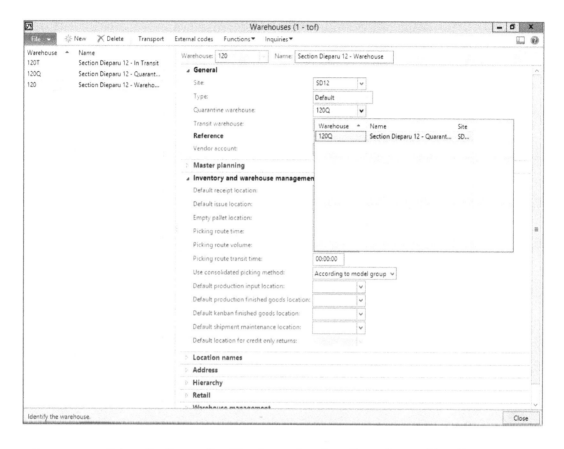

Now you can click on the **Quarantine Warehouse** dropdown list and you will be able to select the **Quarantine** warehouse that you just created.

Assigning In Transit and Quarantine Warehouses To Existing Warehouses

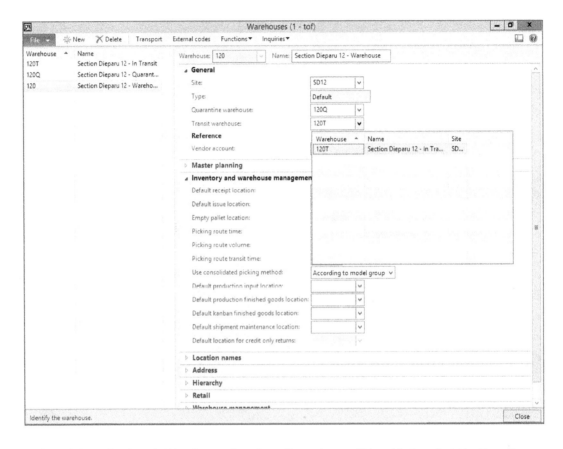

Then click on the **Transit Warehouse** dropdown list and you will be able to select the **Transit** warehouse that you just created.

Assigning In Transit and Quarantine Warehouses To Existing Warehouses

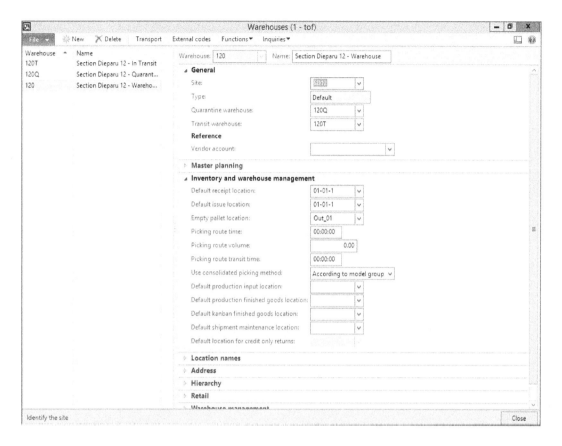

After you have done that you can click on the **Close** button and exit from the form.

Viewing The Inventory Locations Graphically

Now that you have created all of your locations, you can take a little bit of time to admire your work through the graphical location browser.

Viewing The Inventory Locations Graphically

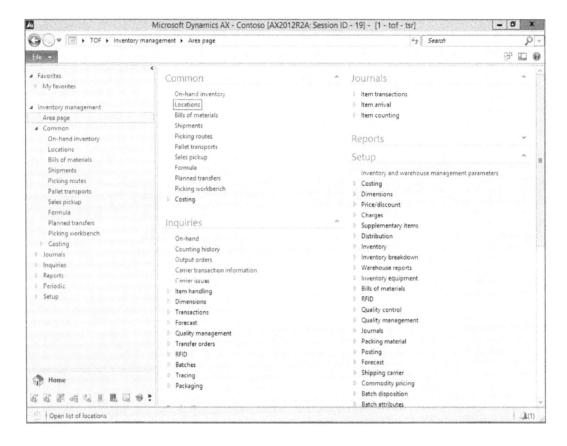

To do this, lick on the **Locations** menu item within the **Common** group of the **Inventory Management** area page.

Viewing The Inventory Locations Graphically

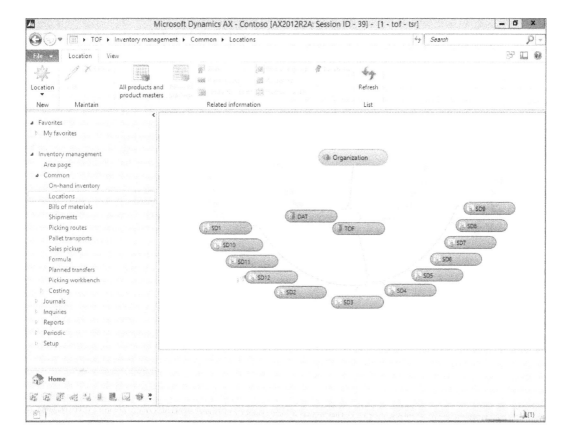

This will open up a browser that shows you all of your companies, and the sites below them.

Viewing The Inventory Locations Graphically

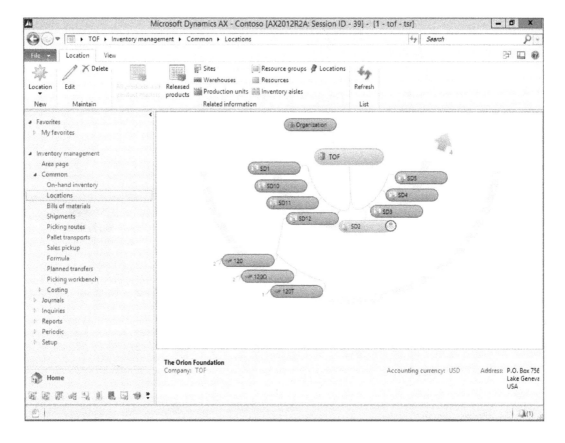

If you click on the **TOF** company then you will be able to see that there are warehouses below the **SD12** site.

Viewing The Inventory Locations Graphically

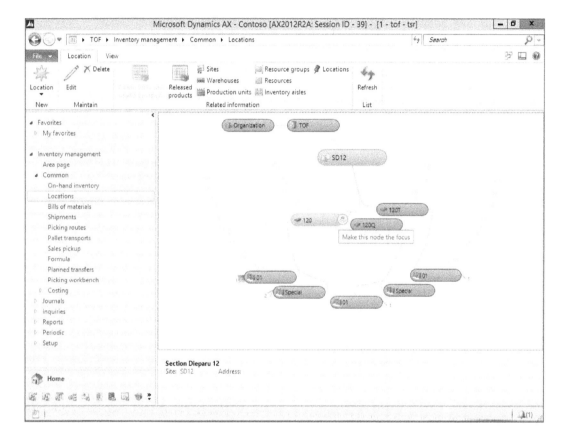

Clicking on the **SD12** site you will drill in even further and see the aisles that you created.

Viewing The Inventory Locations Graphically

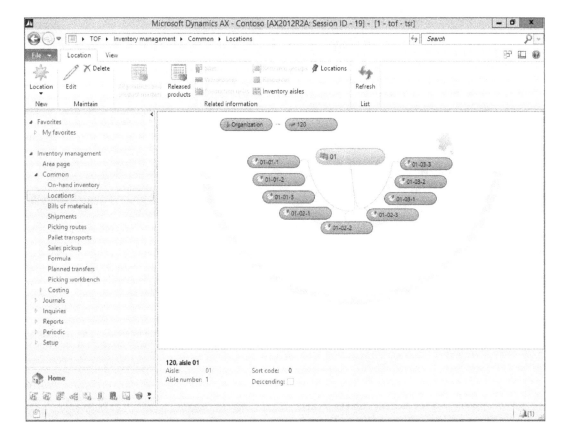

And drilling into the **Aisle** will allow you to see all of the locations that you created. After you have browsed around, you can leave the form.

CONFIGURING PRODUCTS FOR INVENTORY MANAGEMENT

Now that we have our inventory codes and controls configured we can return back to our released products and update them so that they will be able to be managed within the inventory.

Updating Released Products With Inventory Details

The first task that we need to do is to tweak the existing released products a little so that they are able to be used within the inventory management system.

Updating Released Products With Inventory Details

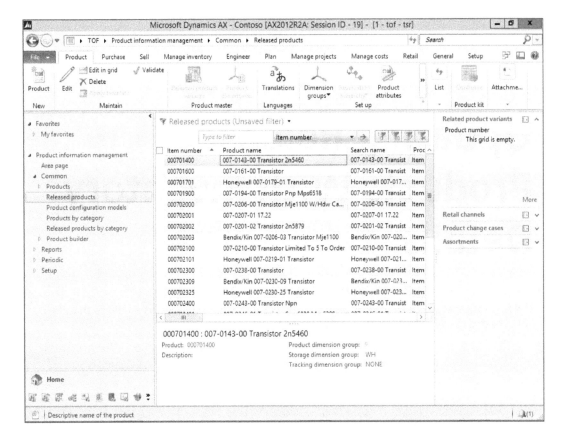

To do this, open up the **Released Products** list page and select the first item in the list.

Updating Released Products With Inventory Details

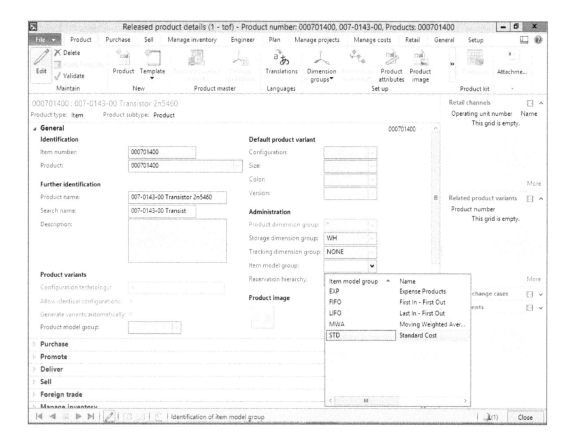

When the **Released Product** detail form is displayed, click on the **Item Model Group** dropdown list and select the inventory model that you want to apply to the product. In this case we will select the **STD** Item Model Group.

Updating Released Products With Inventory Details

Next scroll down and expand out the **Manage Costs** tab group and you will see that there are a few costing fields that we can update.

Updating Released Products With Inventory Details

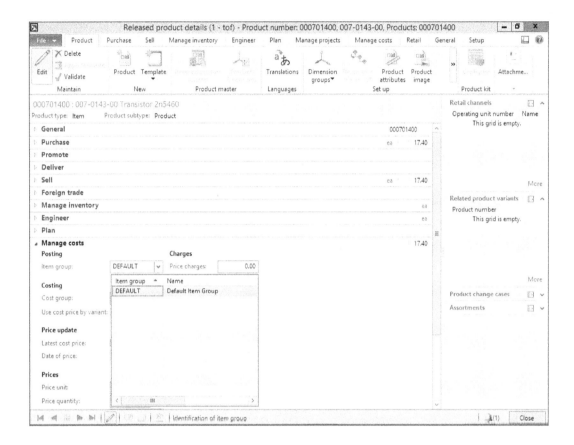

Click on the **Item Group** dropdown list and select the **Default** code so that the item has some default posting profiles associated with it.

Updating Released Products With Inventory Details

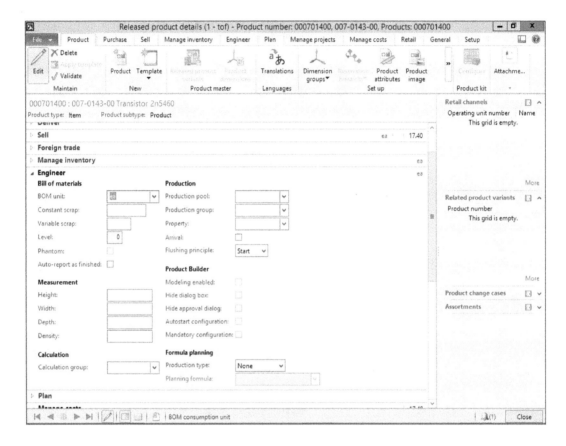

Then expand out the **Engineer** tab group.

Updating Released Products With Inventory Details

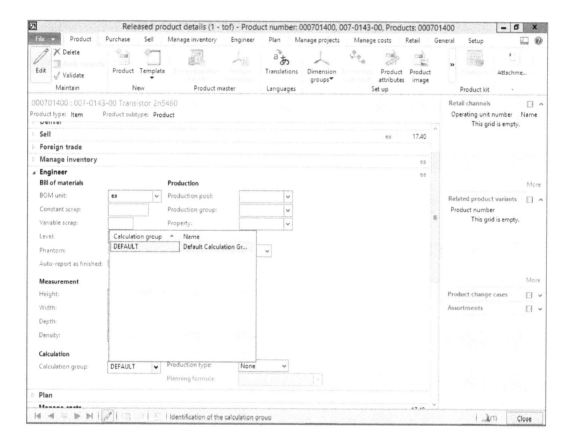

Then click on the **Calculation Group** field and select the **DEFAULT** code that you configured.

Updating The Default Product Costs And Prices

Next we will want to update the product costs so that there will be an active cost for the inventory transactions to post.

Updating The Default Product Costs And Prices

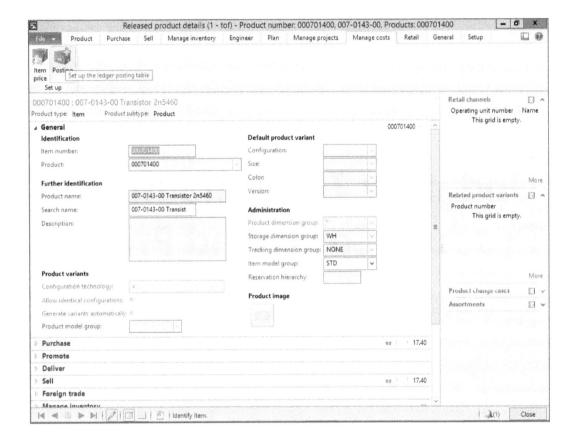

To do this, click on the **Item Prices** button within the **Setup** group of the **Manage Costs** ribbon bar.

Updating The Default Product Costs And Prices

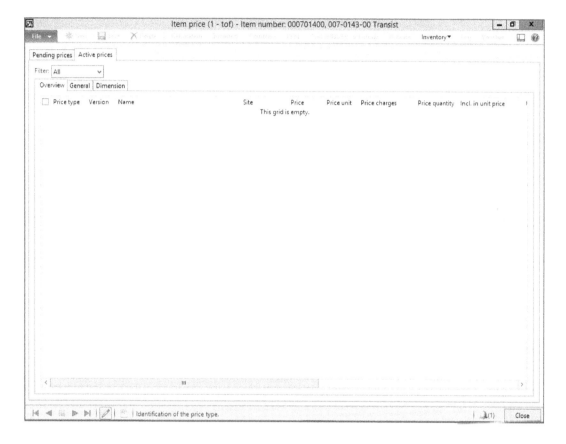

This will open up the **Item Prices** maintenance form and will show you the **Active Prices**. Right now there aren't any so we should set some up.

Updating The Default Product Costs And Prices

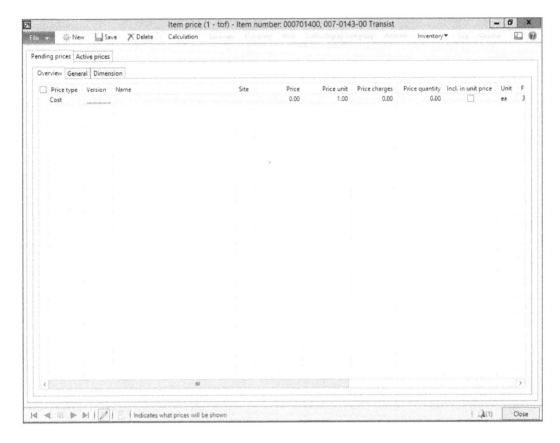

To do this, click on the **ending Prices** tab and that will enable the **Calculation** menu item which you can now click on.

Updating The Default Product Costs And Prices

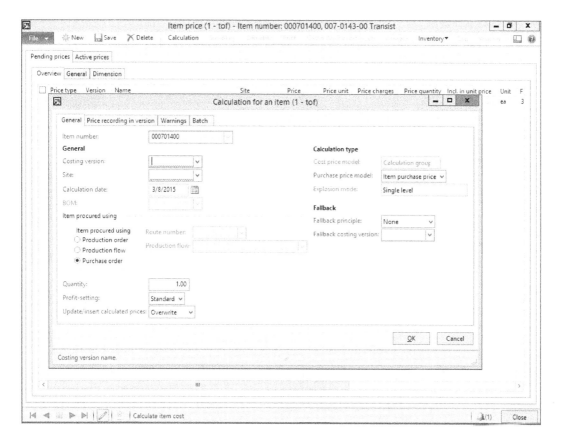

This will open up a **Calculation For An Item** (Cost) dialog box.

Updating The Default Product Costs And Prices

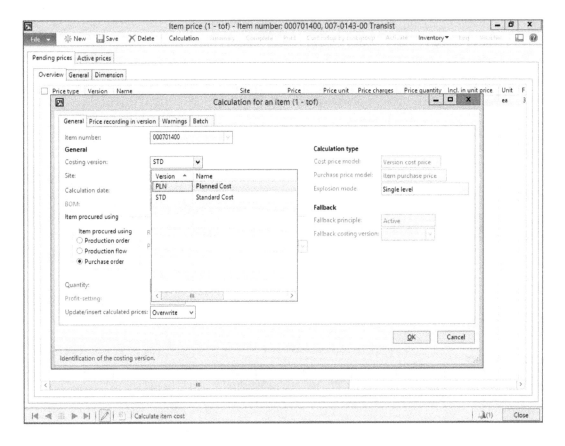

Click on the **Costing Version** dropdown list and select the **STD** costing version.

Updating The Default Product Costs And Prices

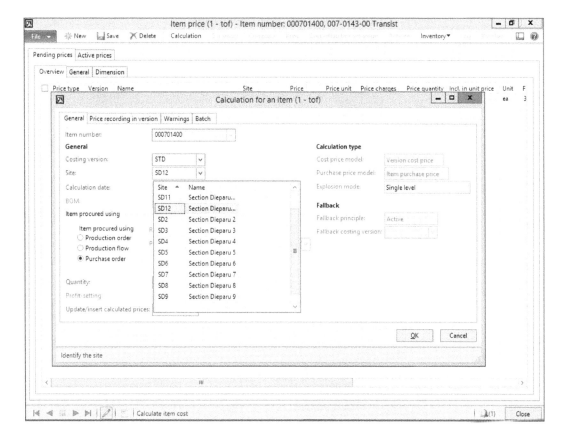

Then click on the **Site** and select the **SD12** site from the dropdown list.

Note: The way that we have the system configured currently allows us to have separate costs by site.

Updating The Default Product Costs And Prices

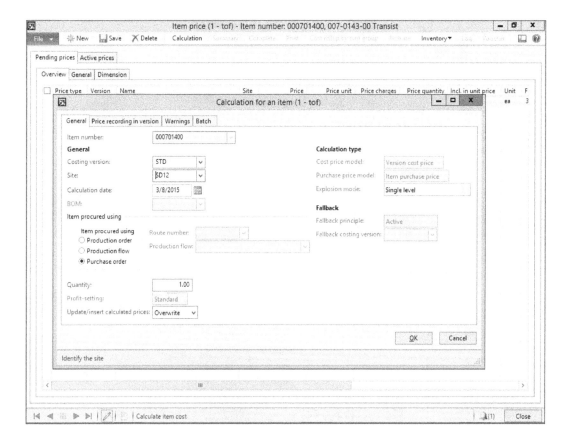

After you have done that, just click on the **OK** button.

Updating The Default Product Costs And Prices

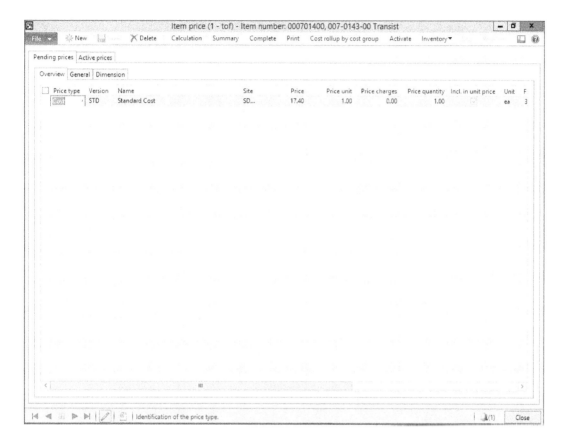

This will create a standard cost for you calculated off the default purchase price of the product. All you need to do is click on the **Activate** button to make it available.

Updating The Default Product Costs And Prices

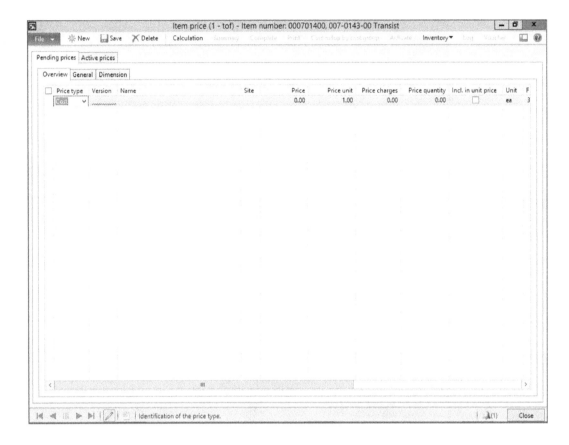

You will notice that the price disappears from the **Pending Prices** tab.

Updating The Default Product Costs And Prices

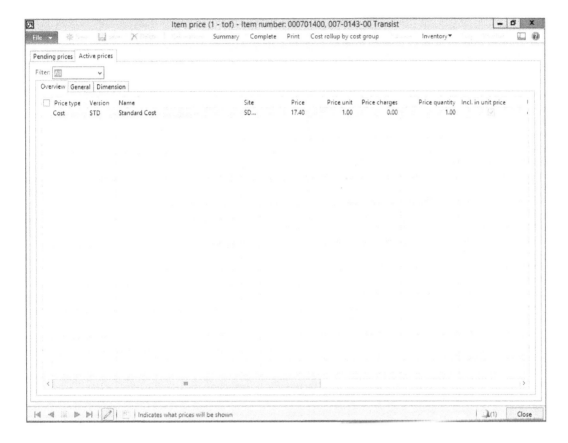

If you click back to the **Active Prices** tab you will now see the price has been posted there.

Now you can just click on the **Close** button and exit from the form.

Performing Mass Updates Through Scripts

If you have more than just a handful of products then you probably don't want to be updating each one by hand to get all of the default information setup for them. You could use Excel to update the products, but if you're feeling a little adventurous then you could save yourself even more time by creating a quick script that does all of the work for you in a fraction of the time.

Performing Mass Updates Through Scripts

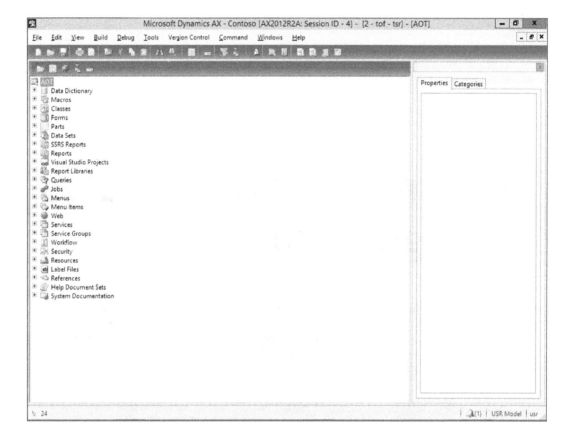

To do this, open up the **AOT** development environment by pressing **CTRL+D**.

Performing Mass Updates Through Scripts

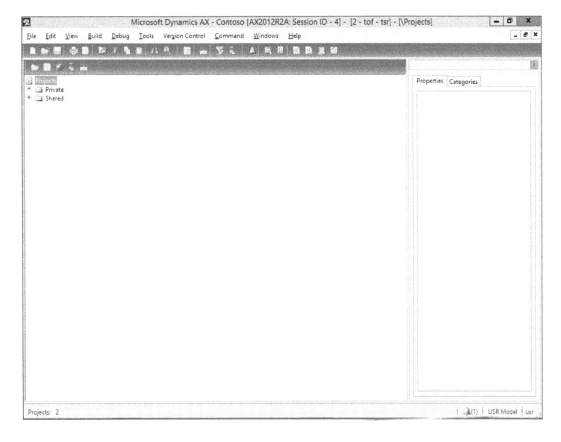

Then open up the **Projects** browser, either by clicking on the icon in the toolbar, or by pressing **CTRL+SHIFT+P**.

Performing Mass Updates Through Scripts

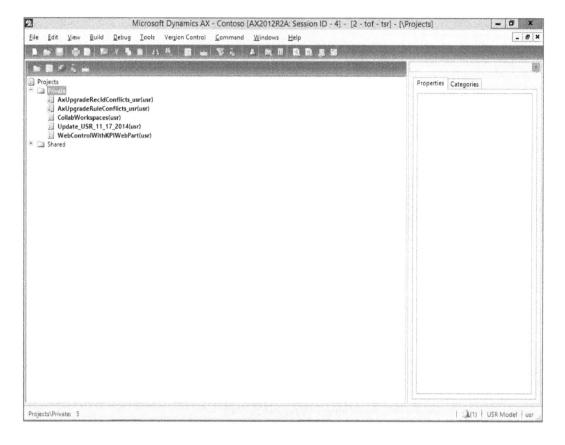

And then expand out the **Private** projects.

Performing Mass Updates Through Scripts

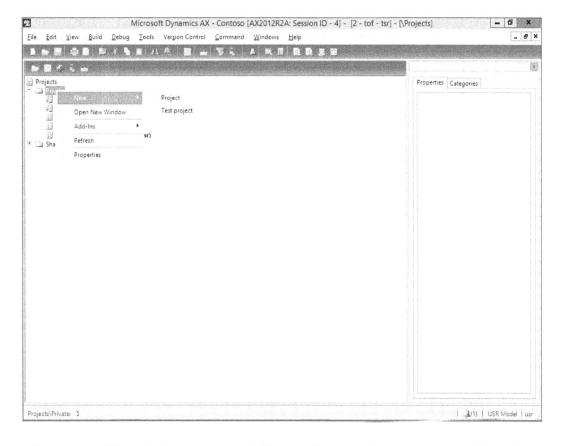

Right-mouse-click on the **Private** projects folder and click on the **New** menu item and then the **Project** submenu item.

Performing Mass Updates Through Scripts

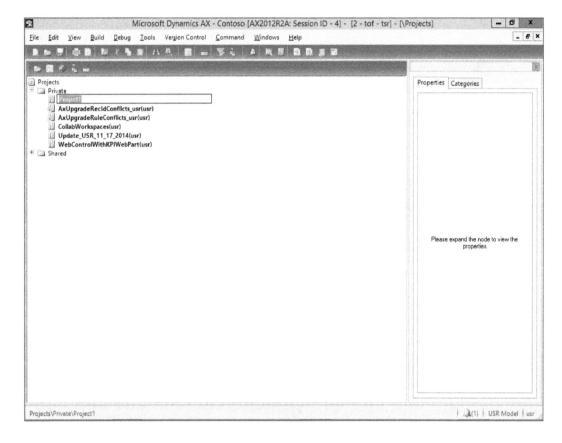

When the project stub is created, double click on it so that you can rename it.

Performing Mass Updates Through Scripts

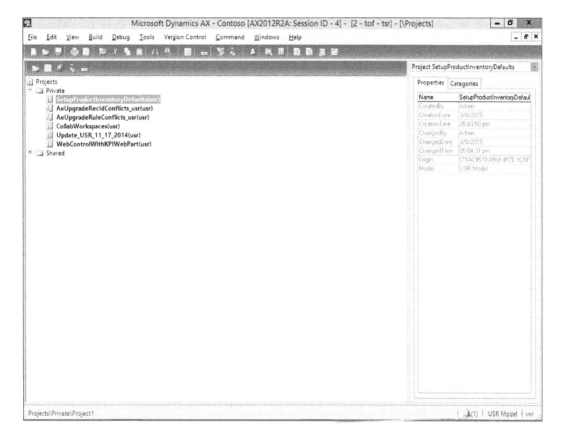

And then set the name to **SetupProductInventoryDefaults**.

Performing Mass Updates Through Scripts

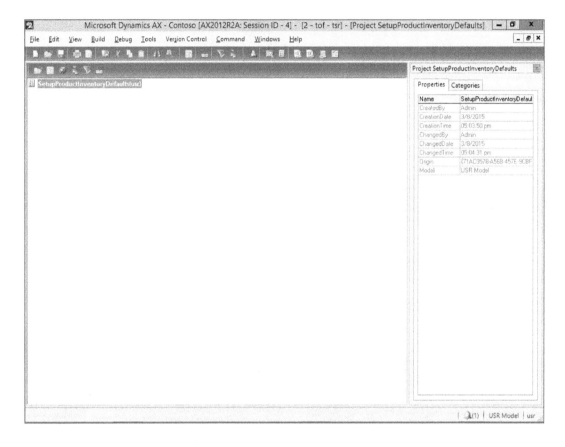

Now right-mouse-click on the new project and select the **Open In New Window** menu item to see just the project.

Performing Mass Updates Through Scripts

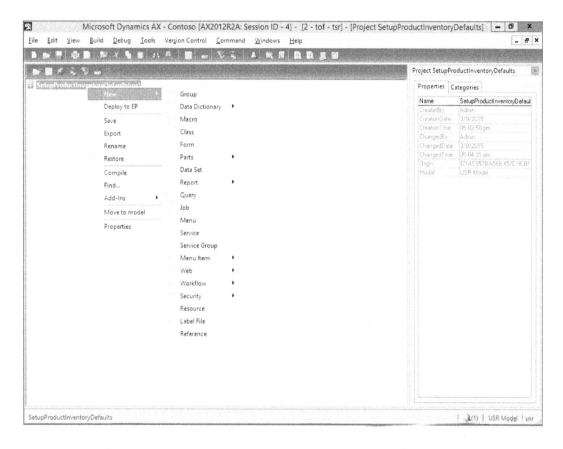

Right-mouse-click on the project name, select the **New** menu item and then select the **Job** sub menu to create a new job script.

Performing Mass Updates Through Scripts

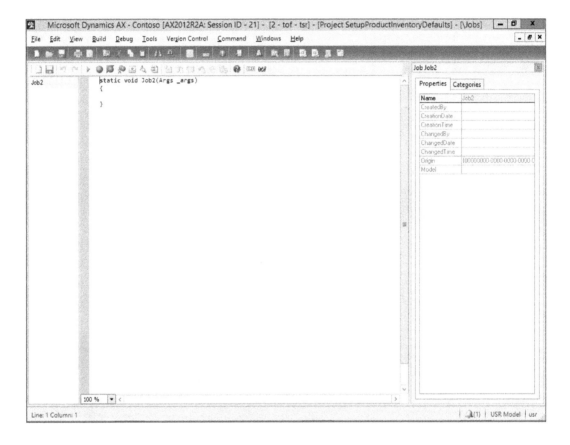

This will open up the X++ editor for the new job.

Performing Mass Updates Through Scripts

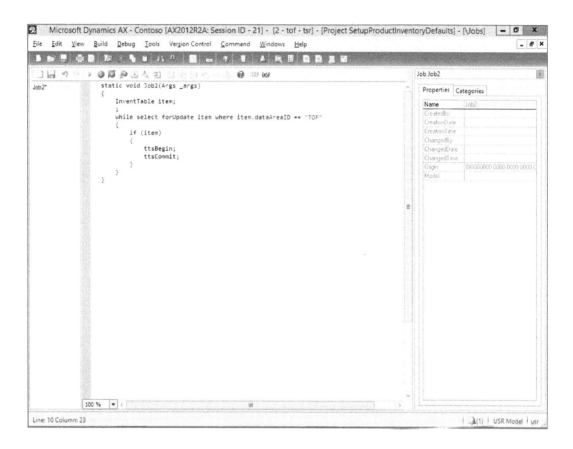

Add the following code to the body of the script:

```
InventTable item;
;
while select forUpdate item where item.dataAreaID == "TOF"
{
  if (item)
  {
    ttsBegin;
    ttsCommit;
  }
}
```

Performing Mass Updates Through Scripts

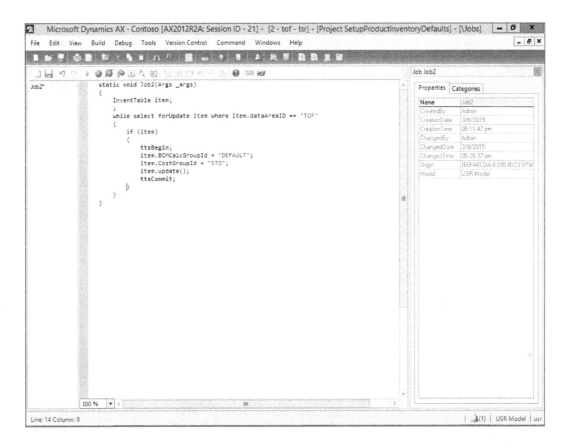

Then within the **ttsBegin** and **ttsComit** statements add this code

```
item.BOMCalcGroupId = "DEFAULT";
item.CostGroupId = "STD";
item.update();
```

This will update the default codes for us.

Performing Mass Updates Through Scripts

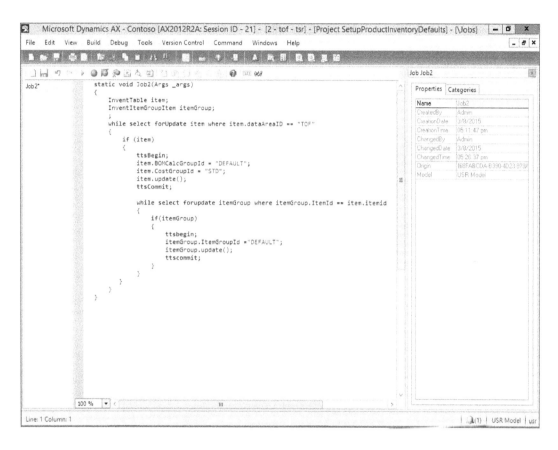

Next we need to update a subtable to set up the Item Group. So add the following line in the header:

```
InventItemGroupItem itemGroup;
```

And this code after the last section of code statement:

```
while select forupdate itemGroup where itemGroup.ItemId == item.itemid
{
  if(itemGroup)
  {
    ttsbegin;
    itemGroup.ItemGroupId ="DEFAULT";
    itemGroup.update();
    ttscommit;
  }
}
```

Performing Mass Updates Through Scripts

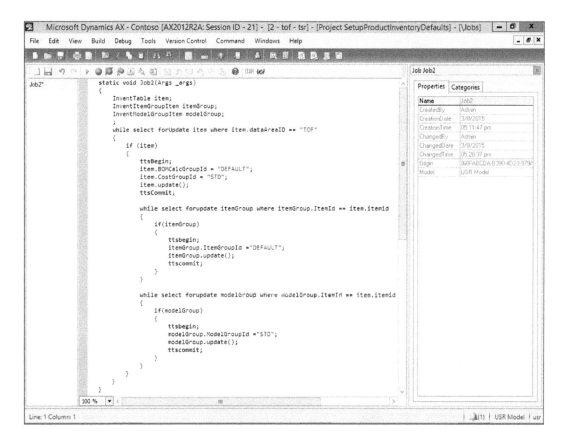

Now we need to tell the system to update the **Model Group** so add the following line in the header:

```
InventModelGroupItem modelGroup;
```

add this code after it:

```
while select forupdate modelGroup where modelGroup.ItemId == item.itemid
{
  if(modelGroup)
  {
    ttsbegin;
    modelGroup.ModelGroupId ="STD";
    modelGroup.update();
    ttscommit;
  }
}
```

Performing Mass Updates Through Scripts

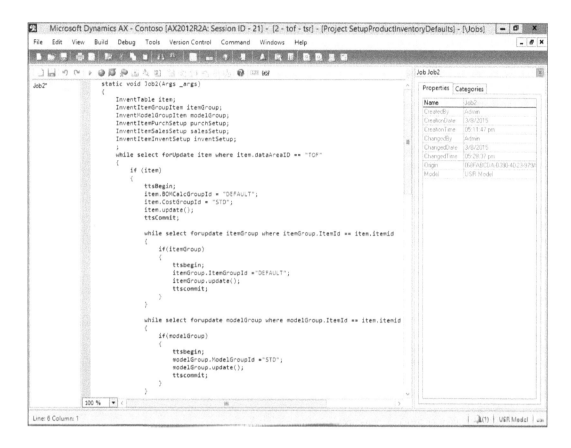

Next we will get the default site details ready to be populated. So add the following line in the header:

```
InventItemPurchSetup purchSetup;
InventItemSalesSetup salesSetup;
InventItemInventSetup inventSetup;
```

Performing Mass Updates Through Scripts

And this code after the last section of code statement:

```
while select forupdate purchSetup where purchSetup.itemid == item.itemid
{
  if(purchSetup)
  {
    ttsbegin;
    purchSetup.InventDimIdDefault ="AllBlank";
    purchSetup.update();
    ttscommit;
  }
}


while select forupdate salesSetup where salesSetup.itemid == item.itemid
{
  if(salesSetup)
  {
    ttsbegin;
    salesSetup.InventDimIdDefault ="AllBlank";
    salesSetup.update();
    ttscommit;
  }
}


while select forupdate inventSetup where inventSetup.itemid == item.itemid
{
  if(inventSetup)
  {
    ttsbegin;
    InventSetup.InventDimIdDefault ="AllBlank";
    inventSetup.update();
    ttscommit;
  }
}
```

Performing Mass Updates Through Scripts

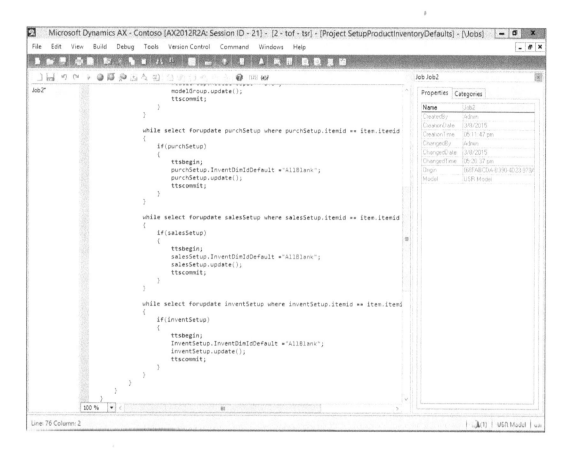

Now your code should look like this.

Performing Mass Updates Through Scripts

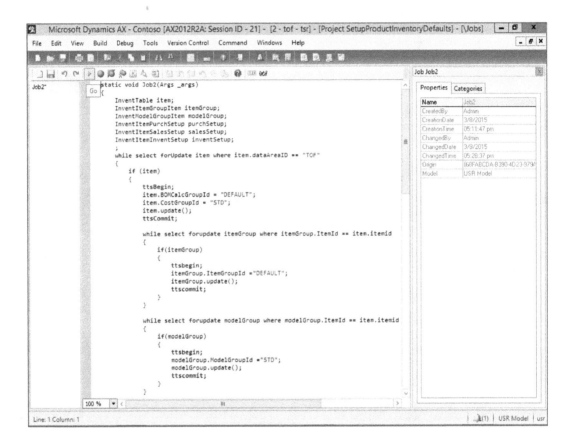

All that you need to do now is to click on the **Run** icon in the ribbon bar.

After a little bit the job will finish and you can exit out of the development environment.

Performing Mass Updates Through Scripts

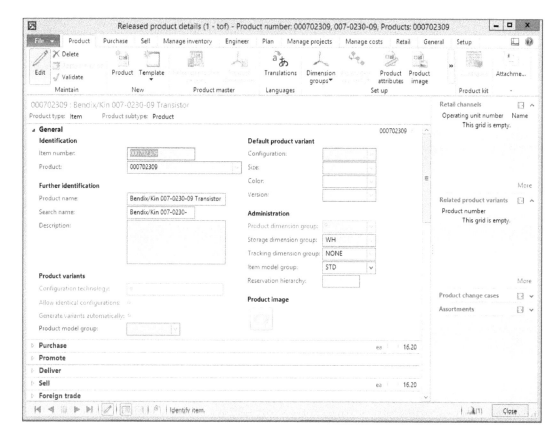

When you return to your released products you will find that they have all been updated for you. How easy is that.

Performing Mass Cost Calculations

Earlier on we performed a cost update for one of the products, but now that we have all of the products updated with the right codes we can be a little more efficient and perform a cost update for all of the products in just one step.

Performing Mass Cost Calculations

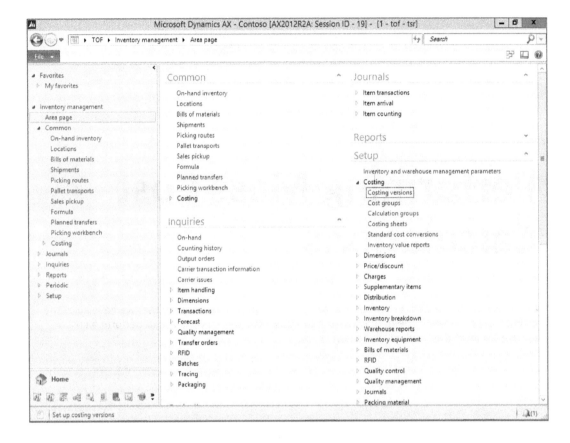

To do this click on the **Costing Versions** menu item within the **Costing** folder of the **Setup** group within the **Inventory Management** area page.

Performing Mass Cost Calculations

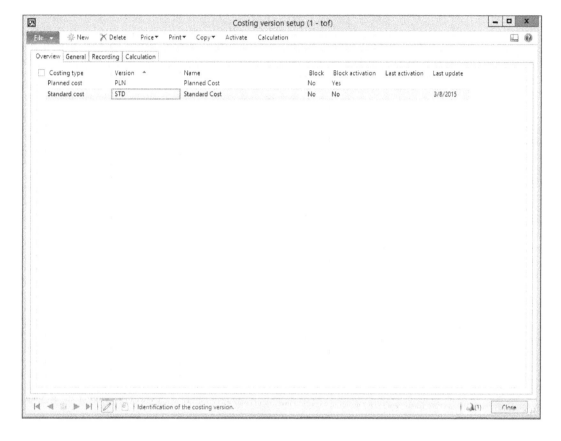

When the **Costing Version Setup** maintenance form is dick on the costing version that you want to perform the update for (we chose **STD**) and then click on the **Calculate** menu item.

Performing Mass Cost Calculations

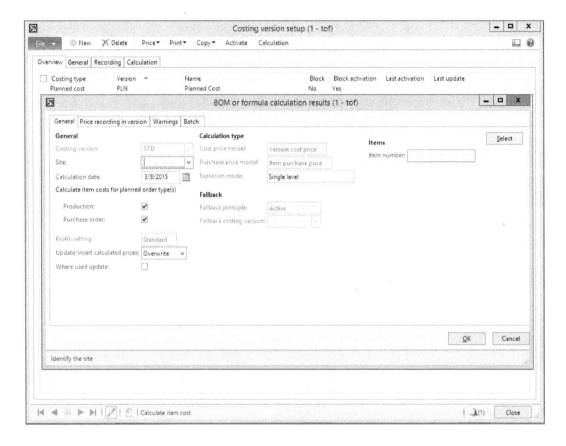

This will open up the **BOM or Formula Calculation Results** form.

Performing Mass Cost Calculations

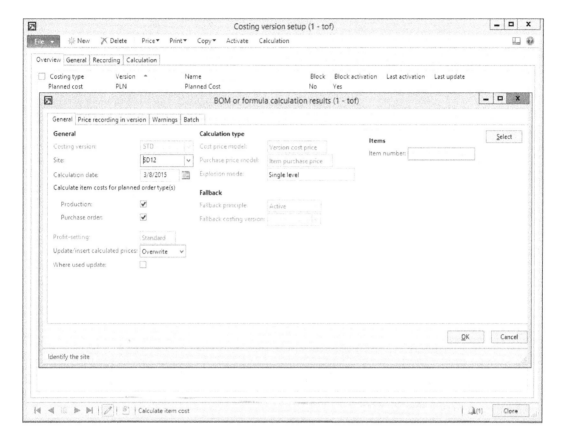

Click on the **Site** dropdown list and select the site that you want to run the update on and then click on the **OK** button.

Performing Mass Cost Calculations

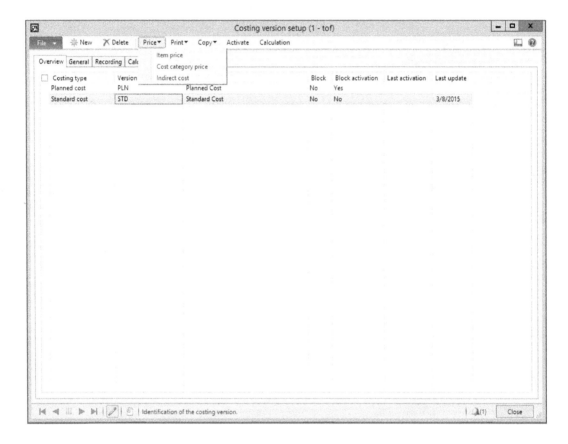

After the update has run, click on the **Prices** menu item in the menu bar and select the **Item Prices** menu item.

Performing Mass Cost Calculations

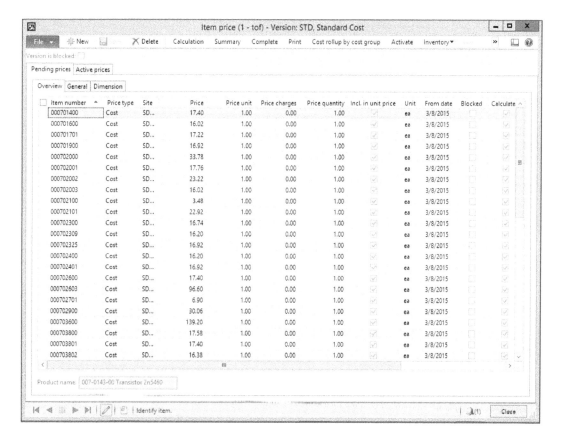

This will show you all of the pending **Item Prices** that were calculated. When you are done, just click the **Close** button to exit from the form.

Performing Mass Cost Calculations

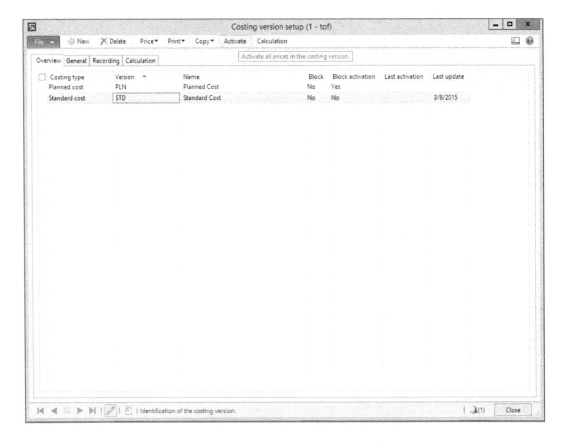

When you return to the **Costing Version Setup** form, click on the **Activate** button in the menu bar.

Performing Mass Cost Calculations

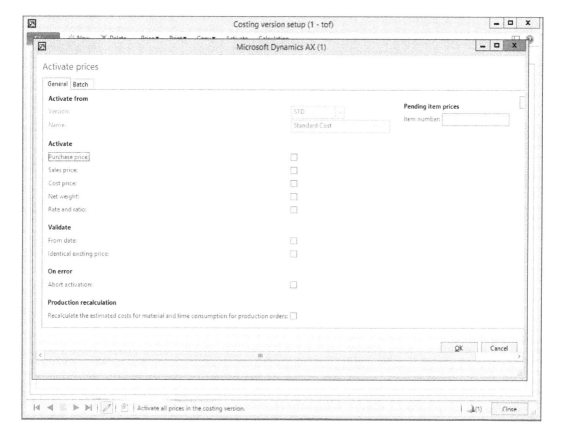

This will open up a **Activate Prices** dialog box where you can select all of the different prices and costs that you want to activate,

Performing Mass Cost Calculations

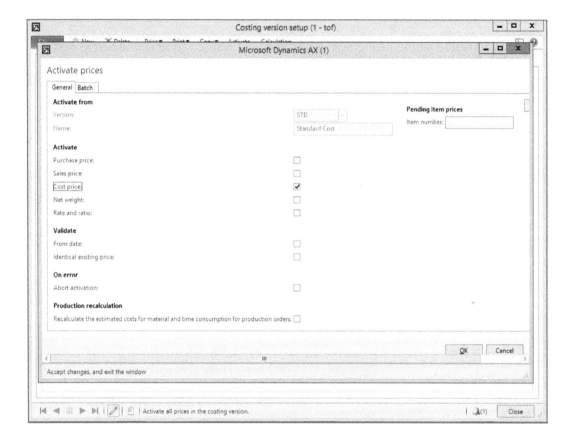

Just check the **Cost Prices** item and then click on the **OK** button.

After the update is completed, you can close out of the forms.

Performing Mass Cost Calculations

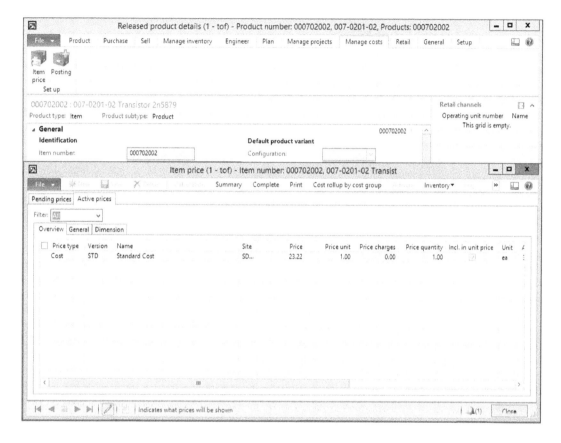

When you return to the **Released Product** if you click on the **Item Price** button within the **Set Up** group of the **Manage Costs** ribbon bar, you will see that all of the costs have been updated for you.

Now that was a lot easier.

Setting The Default Ordering Policies For A Product

If you want to streamline the product even more then you can set up some default ordering policies for your products. This will help default in information for you and also be used later on in modules like the master planning for replenishment.

Setting The Default Ordering Policies For A Product

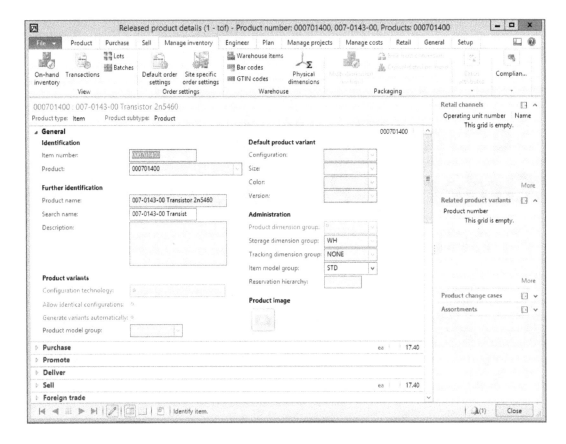

To do this, just open up your released product and then click on the **Default Order Settings** button within the **Order Settings** group of the **Manage Inventory** ribbon bar.

Setting The Default Ordering Policies For A Product

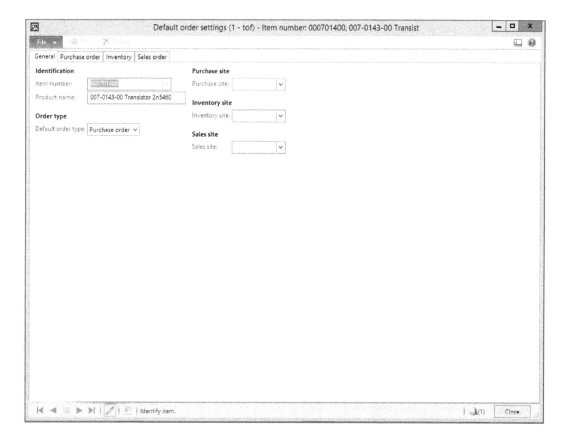

This will open up the **Default Order Settings** maintenance form.

Setting The Default Ordering Policies For A Product

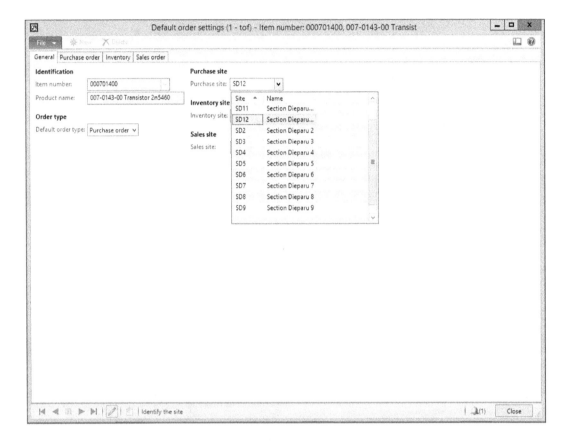

First you can specify the default sites that will use this product. To set up a default purchasing site, click on the **Purchase Site** dropdown list and select the main site that you want to use – in this case we will choose **SD12**.

Setting The Default Ordering Policies For A Product

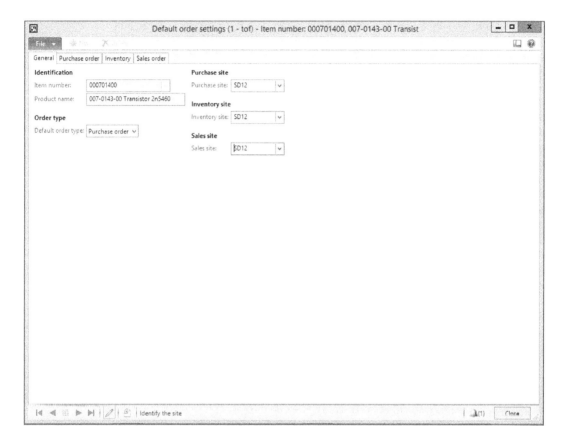

You can then repeat the process for the inventory site by clicking on the **Inventory Site** dropdown list and selecting the **SD12** site, and the **Sales Site** and selecting the **SD12** site.

Setting The Default Ordering Policies For A Product

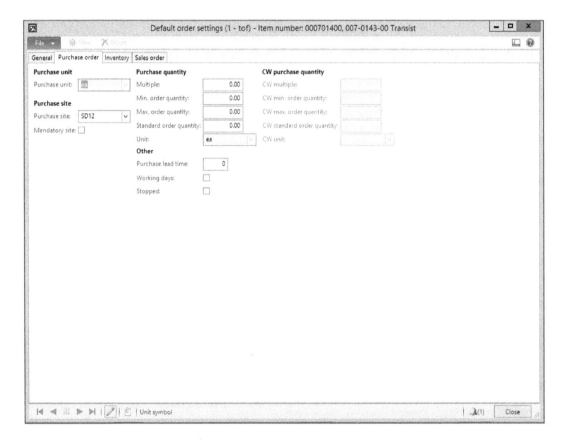

If you click on the **Purchase Order** tab, then you will see all of the default options that will be used when procuring the product.

Setting The Default Ordering Policies For A Product

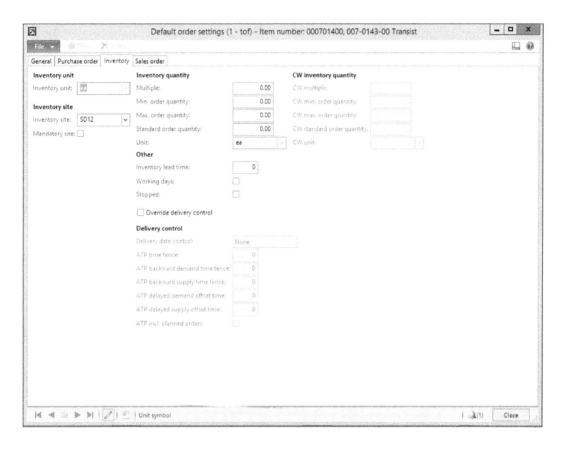

If you click on the **Inventory** tab, then you will see all of the default options that will be used when managing the product within the site, including the ATP windows which you can override here.

Setting The Default Ordering Policies For A Product

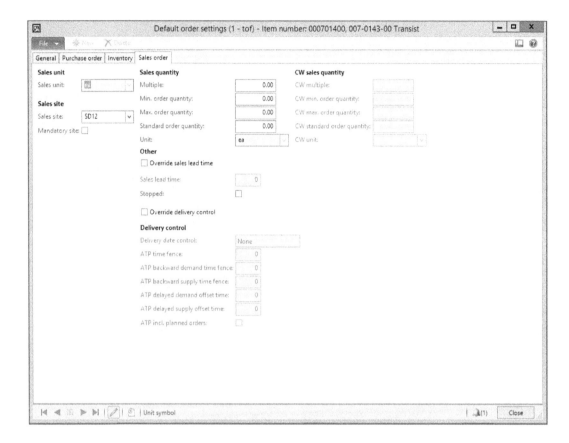

If you click on the **Sales Order** tab, then you will see all of the default options that will be used when selling the product.

After you have checked this out, just click on the **Close** button and you can exit from the form.

Setting Default Order Policies By Site

If you want to get even more granular then you can also set up the default ordering policies by site as well so that each site can treat the products differently.

Setting Default Order Policies By Site

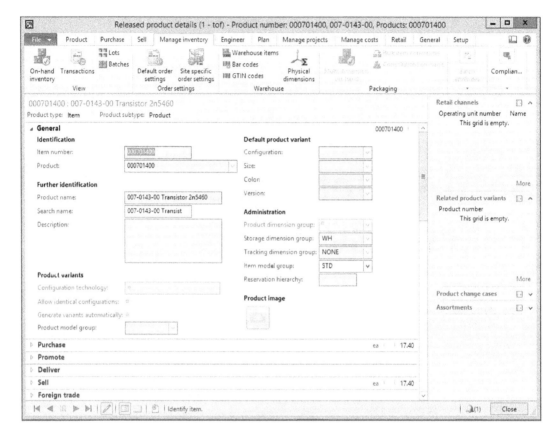

To do this, just open up your released product and then click on the **Site Specific Order Settings** button within the **Order Settings** group of the **Manage Inventory** ribbon bar.

Setting Default Order Policies By Site

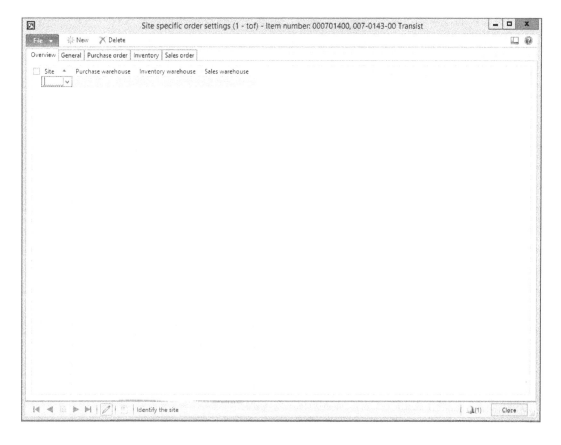

When the **Site Specific Order Settings** maintenance form is displayed, click on the **New** button to add a new record.

Setting Default Order Policies By Site

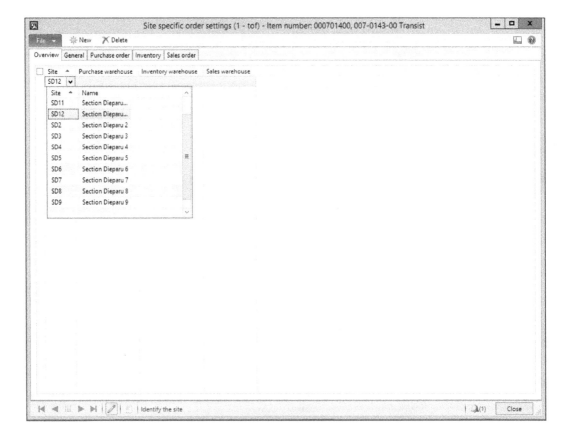

Then click on the **Site** dropdown list and select the site that you want to override the default settings for. In this case we will choose **SD12** again.

Setting Default Order Policies By Site

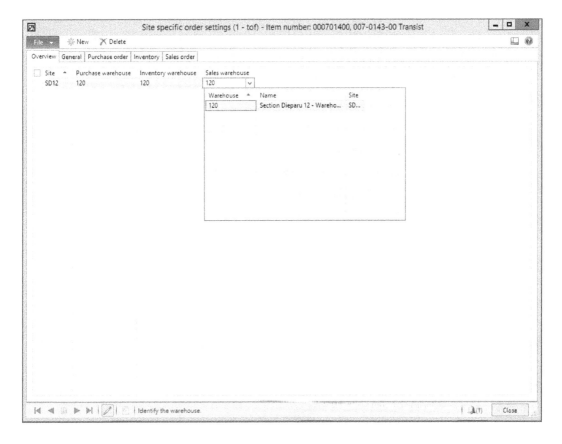

Now you can click on the **Purchase Warehouse**, the **Inventory Warehouse** and the **Sales Warehouse** dropdowns and select the default warehouses that will be used by each of those areas.

Setting Default Order Policies By Site

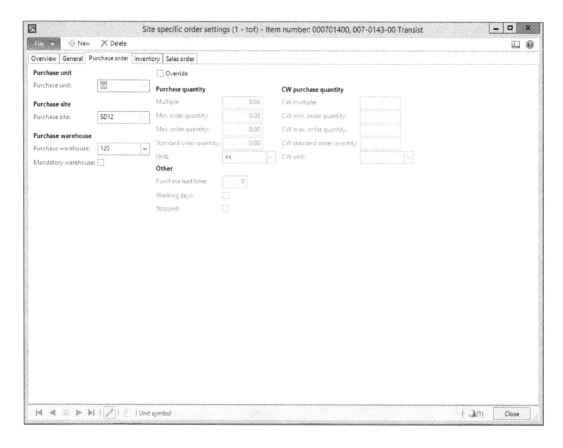

If you click on the **Purchase Order** tab then you will be able to further refine the purchasing policies for the site.

Setting Default Order Policies By Site

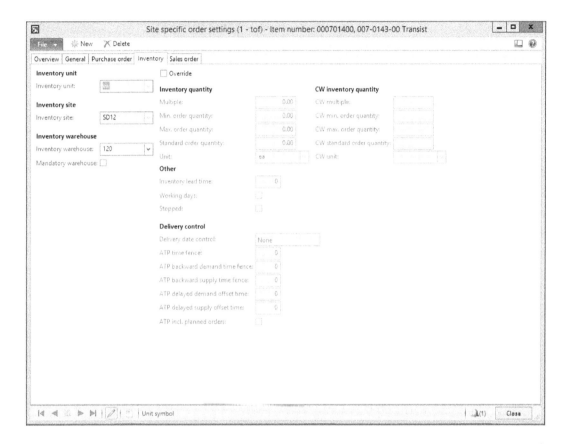

If you click on the **Inventory** tab then you will be able to further refine the inventory policies for the site.

Setting Default Order Policies By Site

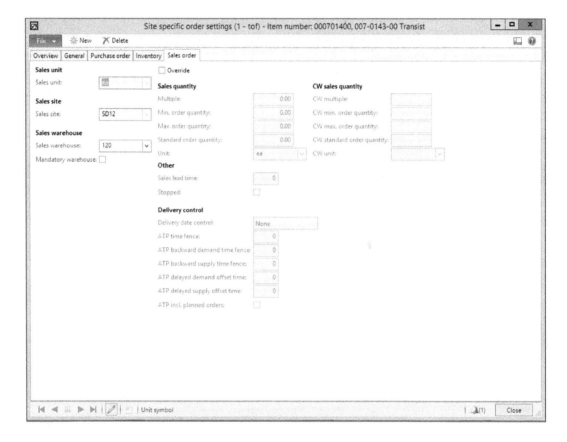

And if you click on the **Sales Order** tab then you will be able to further refine the sales policies for the site.

When you are done, just click on the **Close** button to exit from the form.

CONFIGURING INVENTORY COUNTING

Once you have all of your locations and products configured, you can start performing some transactions within the warehouse. One of the first tasks will probably be to perform an inventory count to get all of your balances up to date.

In this section we will show you how to configure your counting policies and also how to perform cycle counts.

Configuring Inventory Counting Groups

Before we start performing out Cycle Counts though you may want to segregate out the inventory into different counting groups so that you can treat high and low volume products efficiently. To start doing this we will want to set up some **Counting Groups**.

Configuring Inventory Counting Groups

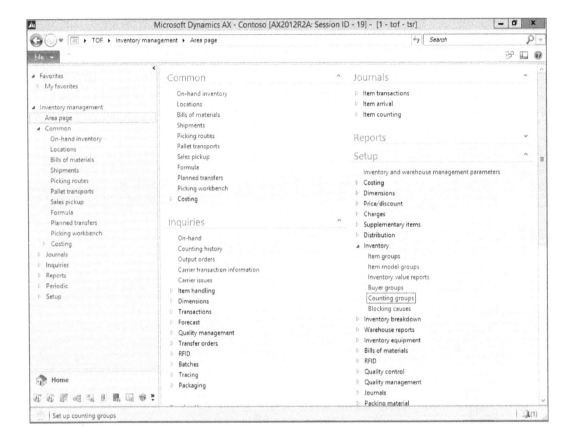

To do this, click on the **Counting Groups** menu item within the **Inventory** folder of the **Setup** group within the **Inventory Management** area page.

Configuring Inventory Counting Groups

When the **Counting Groups** maintenance form is displayed, click on the **New** button in the menu bar to create a new record.

Configuring Inventory Counting Groups

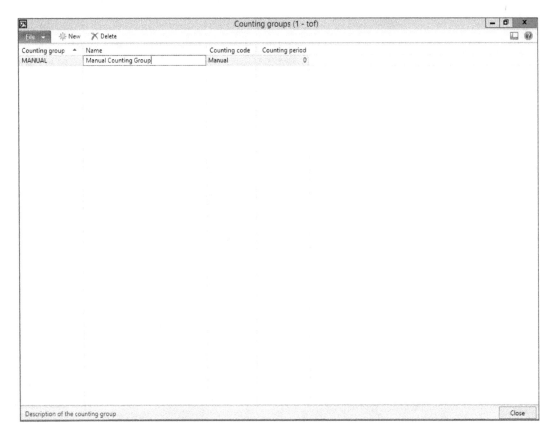

The first counting group that we will create is a for the manual counts. So set the **Counting Group** to **MANUAL** and the **Name** to **Manual Counting Group**.

Configuring Inventory Counting Groups

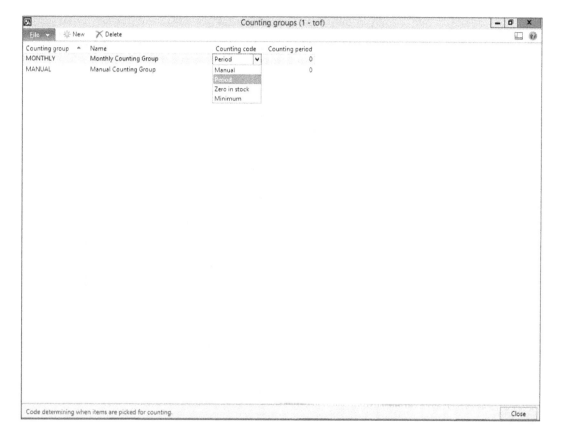

Next we will create a counting group for items that we want to count each month. So click on the **New** button in the menu bar to create a new record, set the **Counting Group** code to **MONTHLY** and the **Name** to **Monthly Counting Group**. Then click on the **Counting Code** dropdown list and select the **Period** option.

Configuring Inventory Counting Groups

Then set the **Counting Period** to **30** (days) – which is close enough to a month for me.

Configuring Inventory Counting Groups

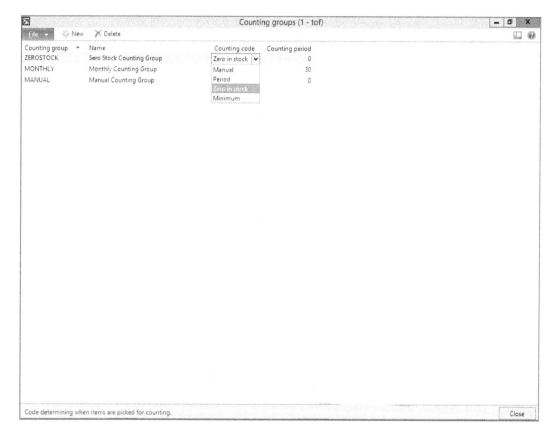

Finally we will create a counting group for items that we want to count when they are supposed to be out of stock. So click on the **New** button in the menu bar to create a new record, set the **Counting Group** code to **ZEROSTOCK** and the **Name** to **Zero Stock Counting Group**. Then click on the **Counting Code** dropdown list and select the **Zero Stock** option.

Configuring Inventory Counting Groups

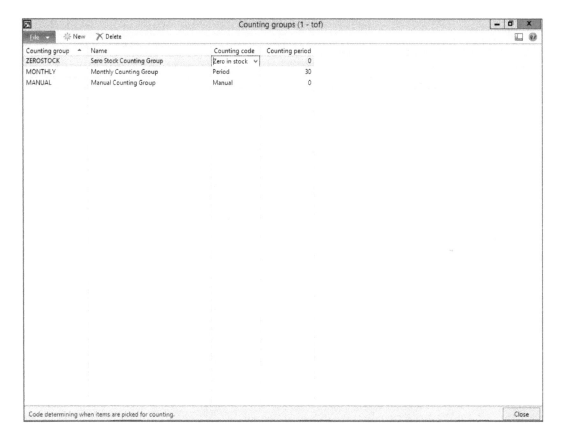

After you have done that you can click on the **Close** button and exit from the form.

Assigning Products To Counting Groups Using Edit In Grid

Since we created the counting groups, we need to now assign them to all of the products. A quick way to do this is to use the **Edit In Grid** feature.

Assigning Products To Counting Groups Using Edit In Grid

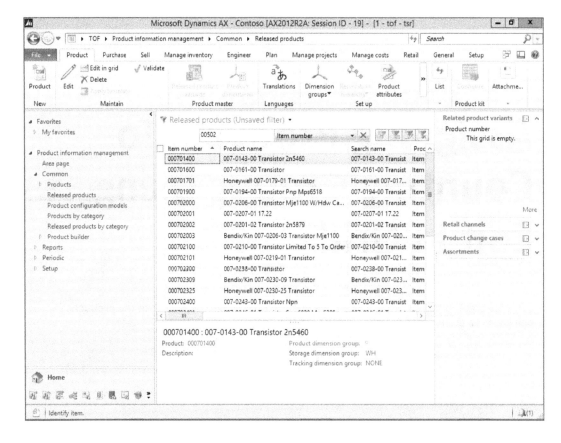

To do this, open up the **Released Products** page as a list page, and then click on the **Edit In Grid** button within the **Maintain** group of the **Product** ribbon bar.

Assigning Products To Counting Groups Using Edit In Grid

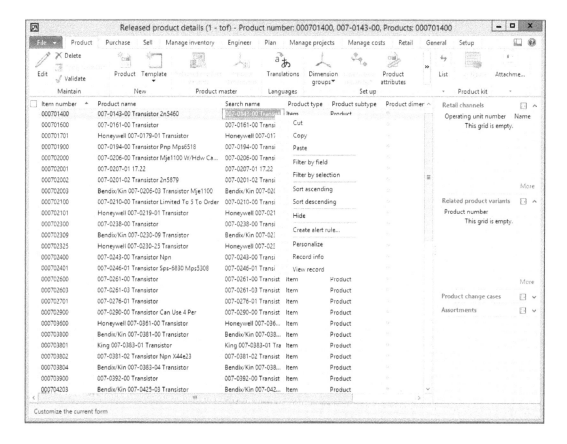

When the **Edit In Grid** form is displayed, right-mouse-click on the form and select the **Personalize** option.

Assigning Products To Counting Groups Using Edit In Grid

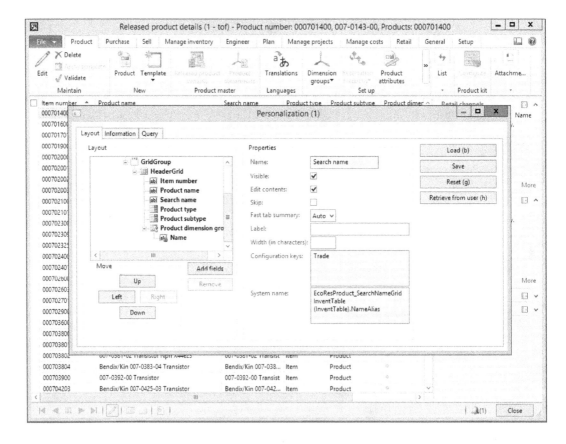

When the **Personalization** form is displayed, we want to add in the **Counting Group** into the form, so click on the **Add Fields** button.

Assigning Products To Counting Groups Using Edit In Grid

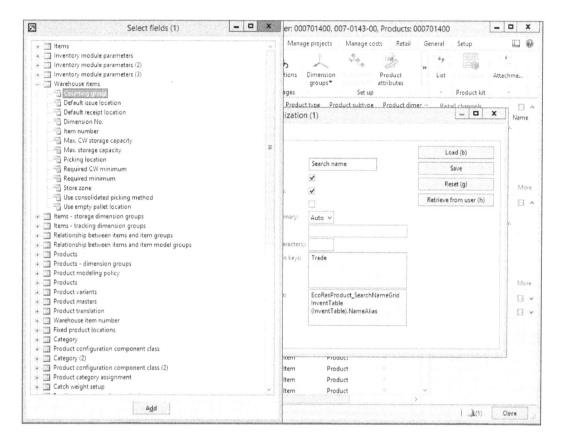

When the **Select Fields** explorer is displayed, expand out the **Warehouse Items** field group and you will see the **Counting Group** field. Select it and then click on the **Add** button at the bottom of the form to add it to the grid. When you are done, just close the **Select Fields** form.

Assigning Products To Counting Groups Using Edit In Grid

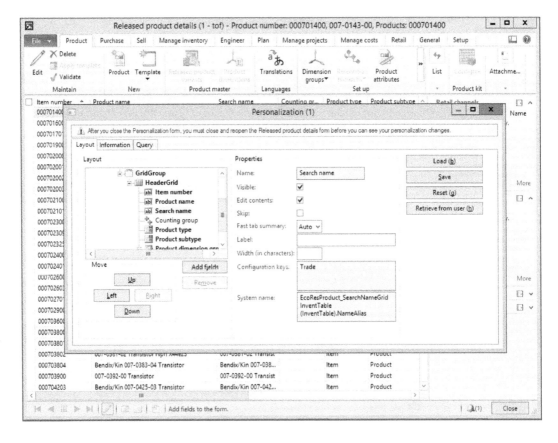

Now you will see that the **Counting Group** field has been added to the form personalization and you can close out of that form as well.

Assigning Products To Counting Groups Using Edit In Grid

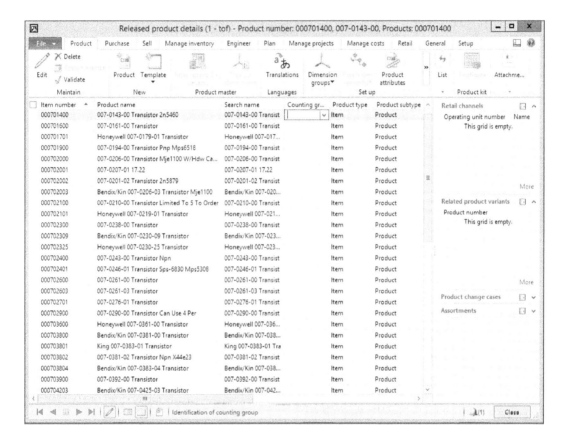

When you return to the **Edit In Grid** view you will see that the **Counting Group** field is now available for you to update.

Assigning Products To Counting Groups Using Edit In Grid

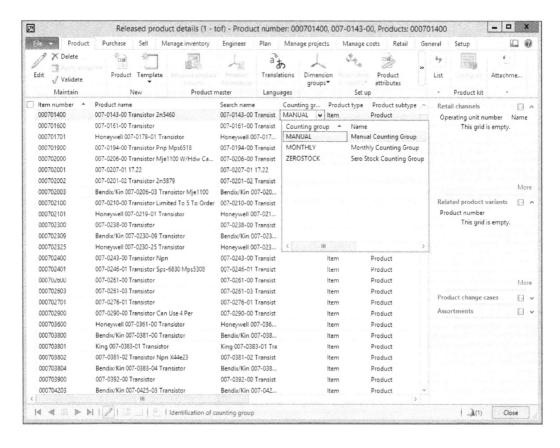

All you need to do is click on the dropdown list and select the counting group that you want to use for the product.

Assigning Products To Counting Groups Using Edit In Grid

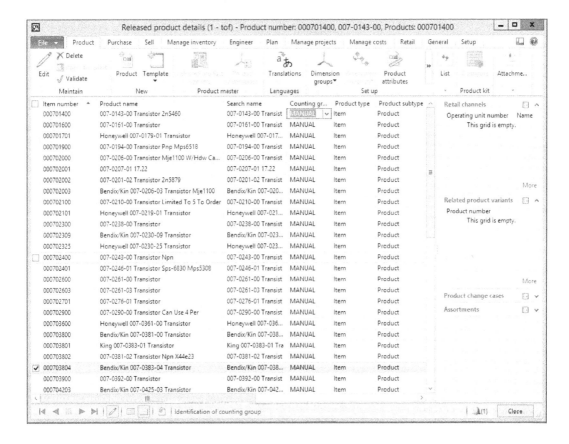

And then repeat the process for all of the other products.

When you are done, just click on the **Close** button to exit from the form.

Creating A Cycle Count

Now we are ready to create our first Cycle Count.

Creating A Cycle Count

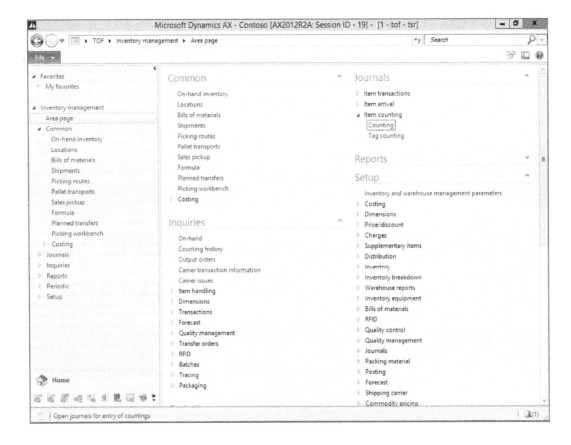

To do this, click on the **Counting** menu item within the **Item Counting** folder of the **Journals** group within the **Inventory Management** area page.

Creating A Cycle Count

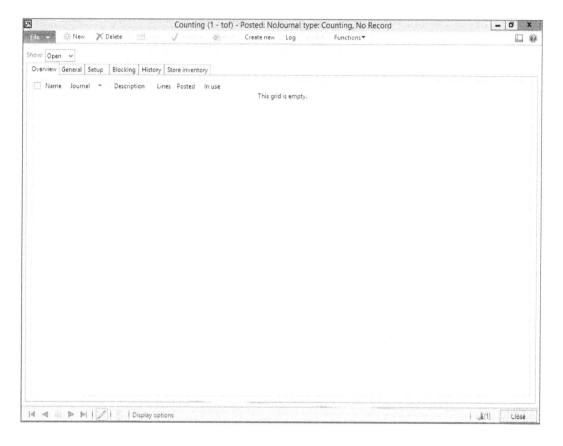

When the **Counting** list page is displayed, click on the **New** button to create a new count.

Creating A Cycle Count

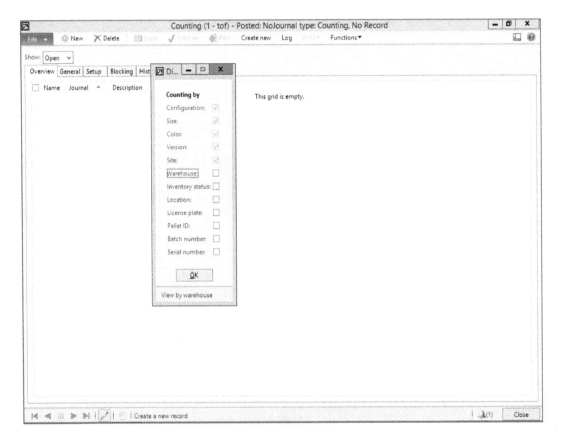

The first time that you perform a count though the **Inventory Dimensions** dialog will be displayed, asking you what level you want to count to.

Creating A Cycle Count

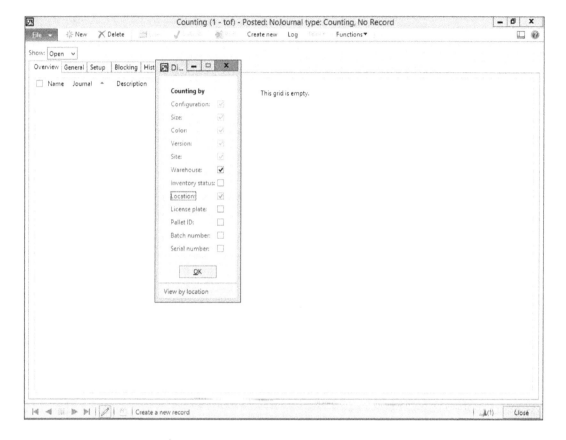

Select the **Warehouse** and the **Location** flags and then click on the **OK** button.

Creating A Cycle Count

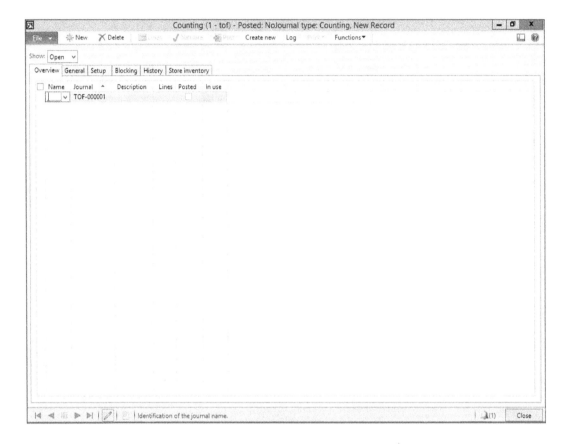

Now you are really ready to start.

Creating A Cycle Count

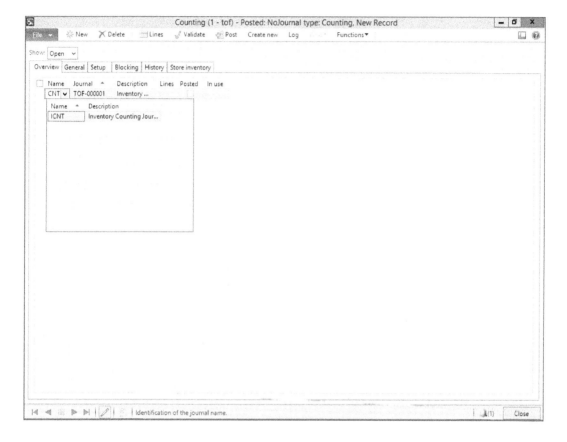

Click on the **Name** dropdown and select the **ICNT** inventory movement type.

Then click on the **Lines** button in the menu bar.

Creating A Cycle Count

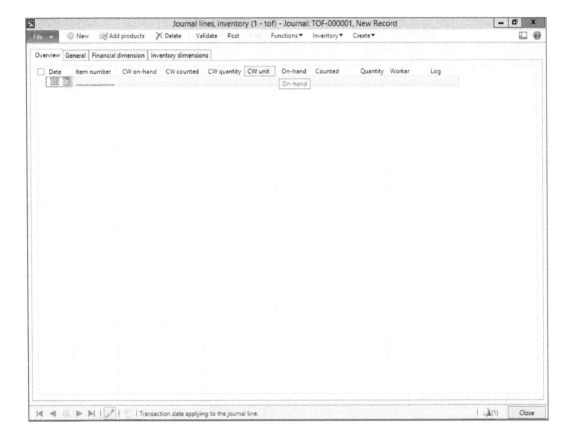

This will open up the **Journal Lines** list page. You can manually create your count lines here if you want...

Creating A Cycle Count

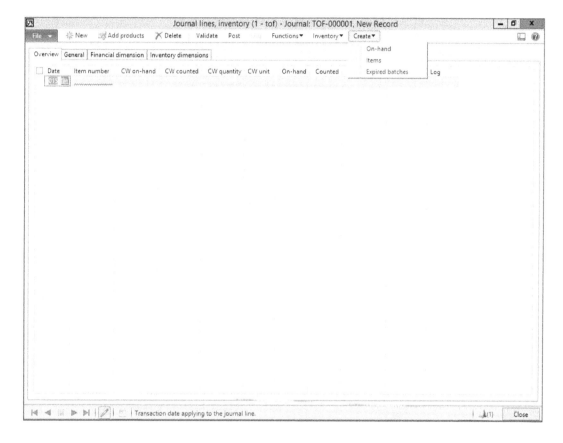

Although if you want the system to suggest the items to be counted, then click on the **Create** button in the menu bar and select the **Items** menu item.

Creating A Cycle Count

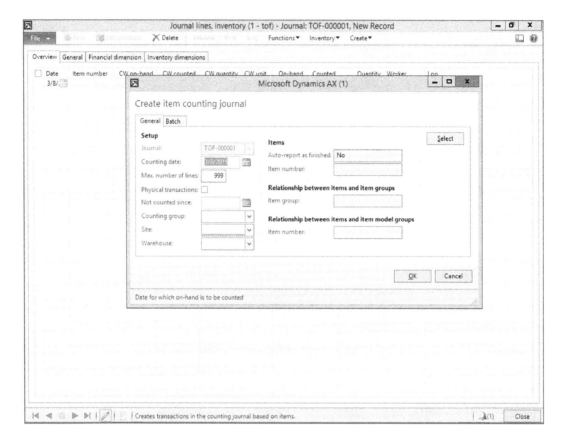

This will open up a **Create Item Counting Journal** dialog box where you an specify what products you want to select for the count.

Creating A Cycle Count

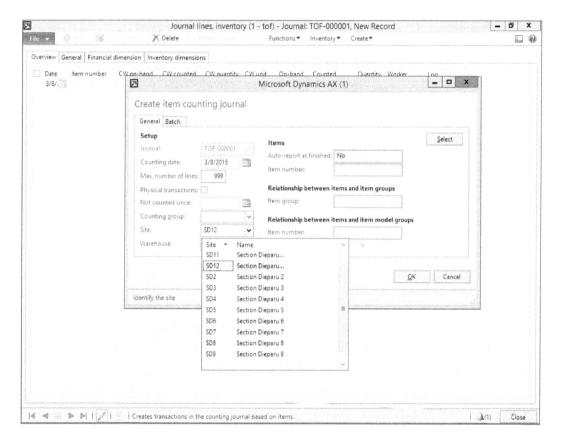

Click on the **Site** dropdown list and select **SD12** from the list to indicate that we want to count just that site.

Creating A Cycle Count

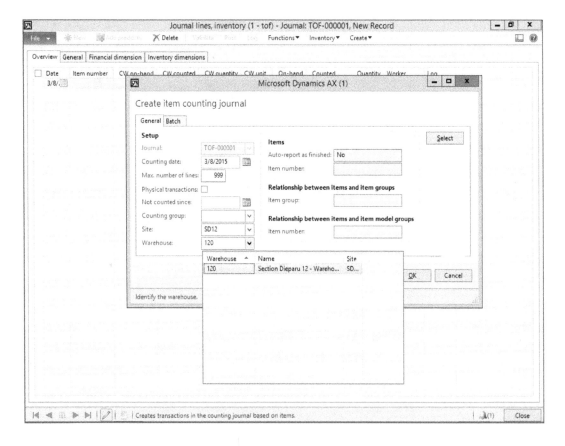

Then click on the **Warehouse** dropdown list and select the warehouse that we want to create the count for. In this case we selected the **120** warehouse.

Creating A Cycle Count

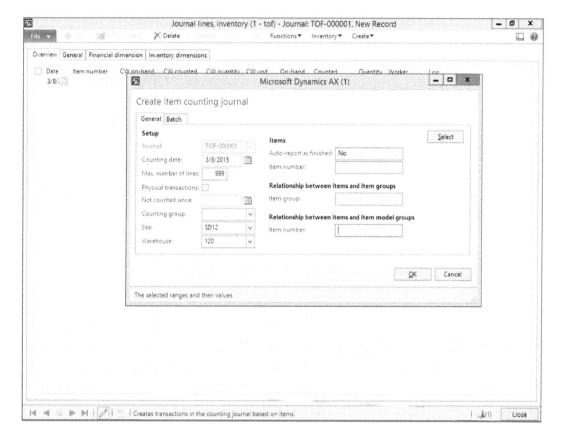

We can further refine the selection if we like, but for now we will just do a complete physical so click on the **OK** button.

Creating A Cycle Count

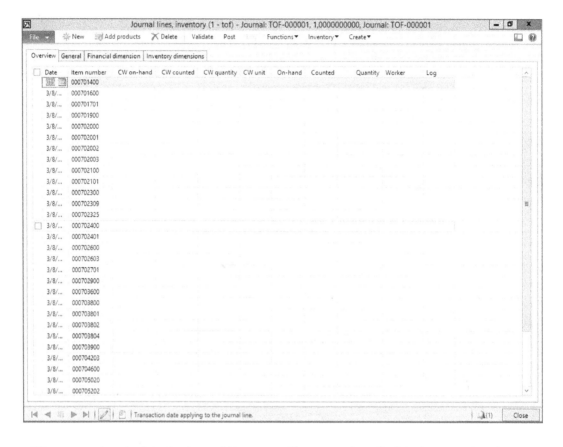

When you return back to the **Journal Lines** you will now see that all of the item numbers have been added to our count.

Creating A Cycle Count

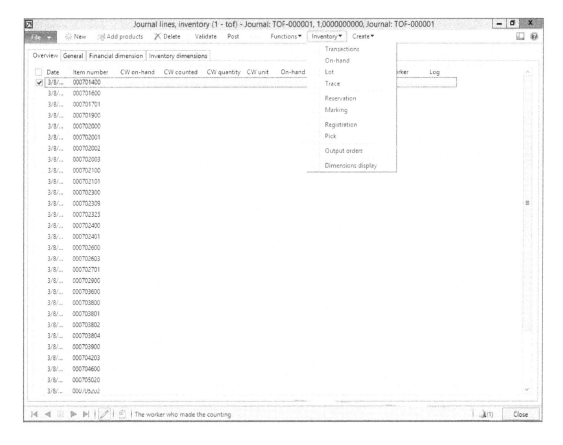

One thing that you will notice though is that the **Site**, **Warehouse** and **Location** are not showing up ion the form. We can fix that by clicking on the **Inventory** button in the menu bar and selecting the **Dimension Display** menu item.

Creating A Cycle Count

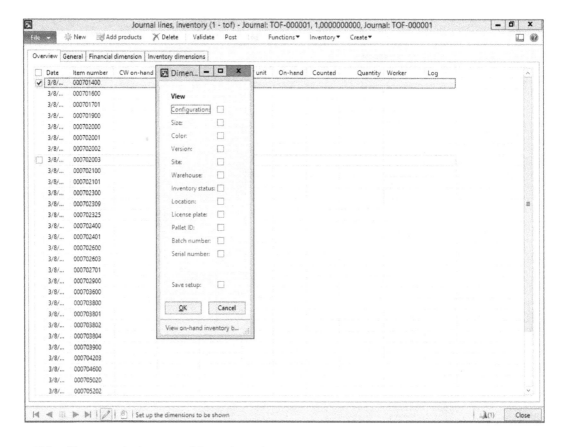

This will pop up the inventory **Dimension** selector.

Creating A Cycle Count

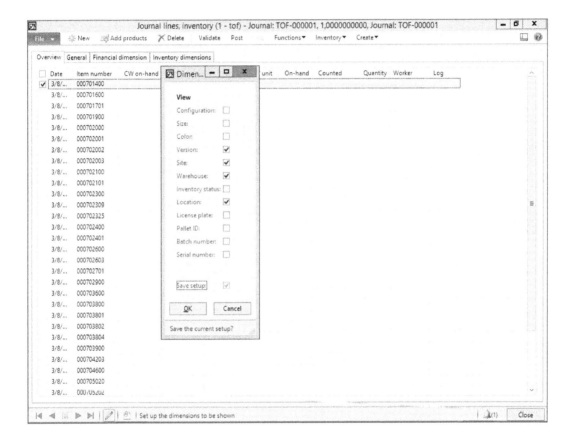

Click on the **Version**, **Site**, **Warehouse** and **Location** inventory dimensions, and then click on the **Save Setup** flag to make this the standard for the form and then click the **OK** button

Creating A Cycle Count

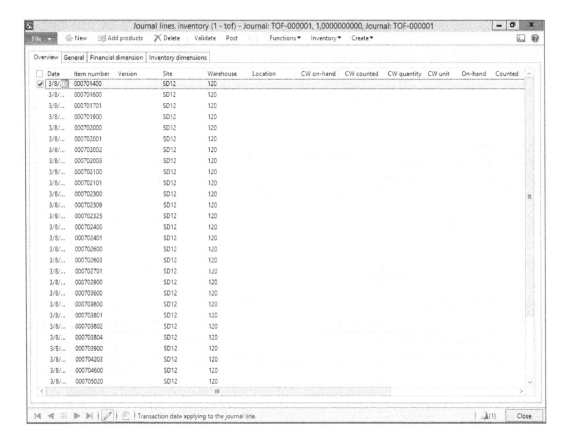

Now when we look at the form we will see a little bit more information is there.

Creating A Cycle Count

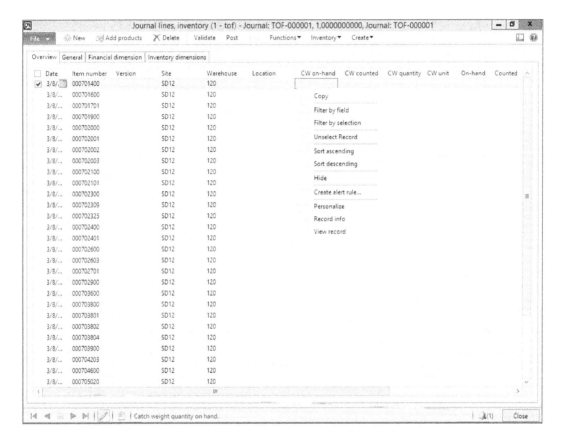

If you want to clean up the form a little then you can right-mouse-click on the **CW On Hand** field and select the **Hide** option. This will hide the catch weight field which we are not using right now. Repeat that process for all of the CW fields.

Creating A Cycle Count

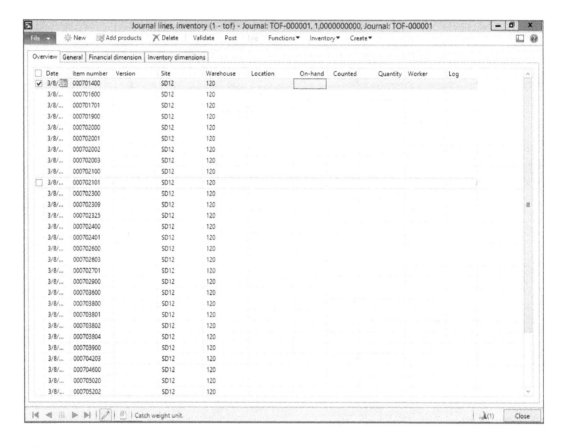

Now you have a much tidier counting list page.

Creating A Cycle Count

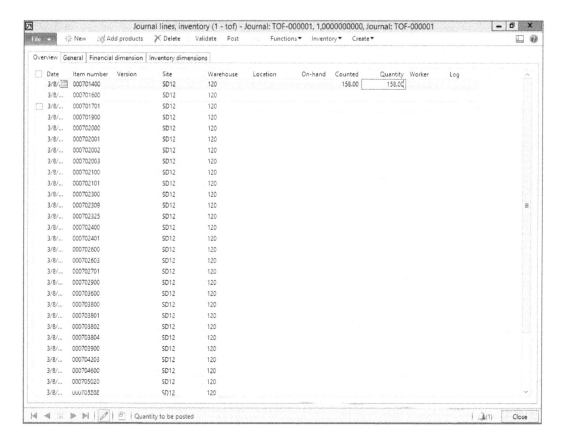

To record a count, just type in the count into the **Quantity** field.

Creating A Cycle Count

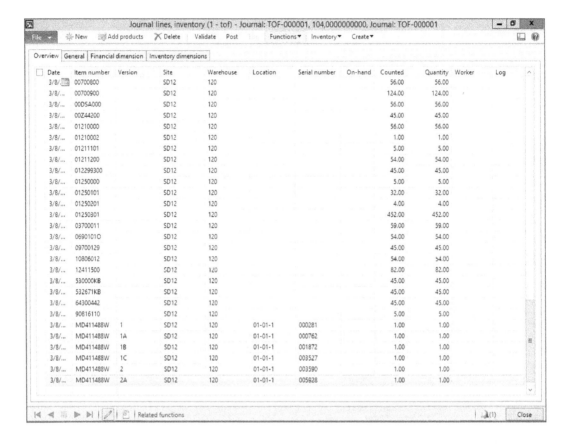

Now count the rest of the inventory the same way.

When you are done, click on the **Validate** button to check that the count has been fully updated.

Creating A Cycle Count

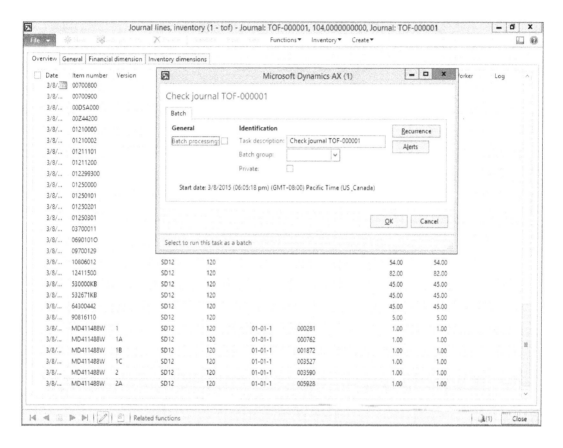

This will open up a **Check Journal** dialog box/ Just click the **OK** button.

Creating A Cycle Count

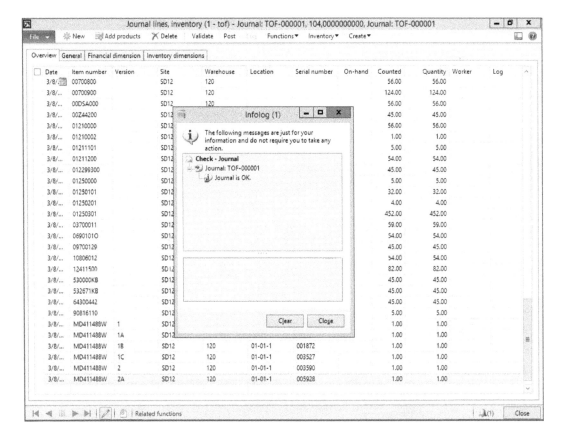

If everything was updated within the count then you will get an InfoLog that says that the journal was updated and you can close out of the form.

Now you can click on the **Post** button within the menu bar to post the count for real.

Creating A Cycle Count

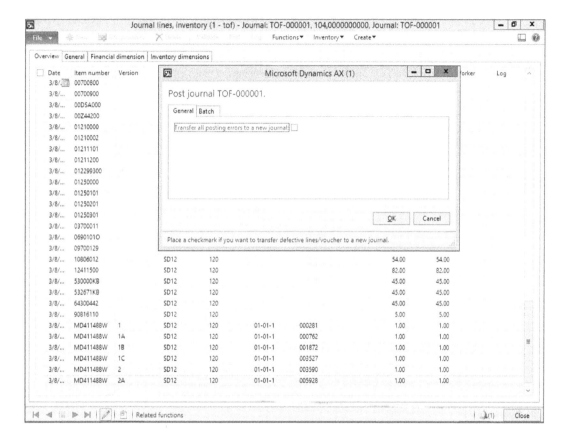

This will open up a **Post Journal** dialog box. Just click on the **OK** button to continue the update.

Creating A Cycle Count

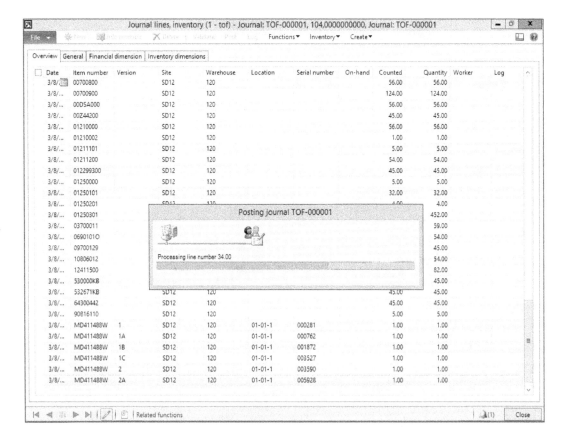

The system will now process all of the inventory updates for you.

Creating A Cycle Count

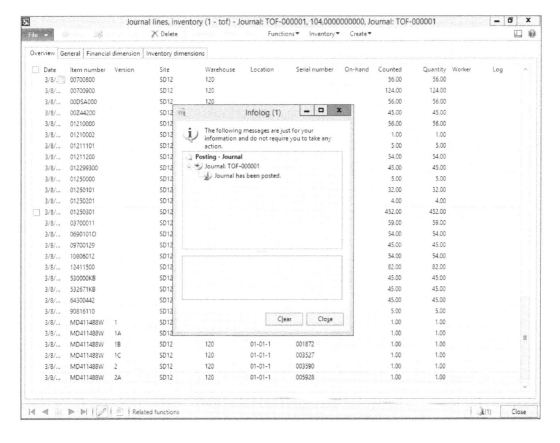

After the count has been updated, you will get an InfoLog and you can close out of that and then click on the **Close** button on the count as well to exit out of that form.

Viewing On Hand Inventory

Now that we have inventory we can start looking at the inventory balances.

Viewing On Hand Inventory

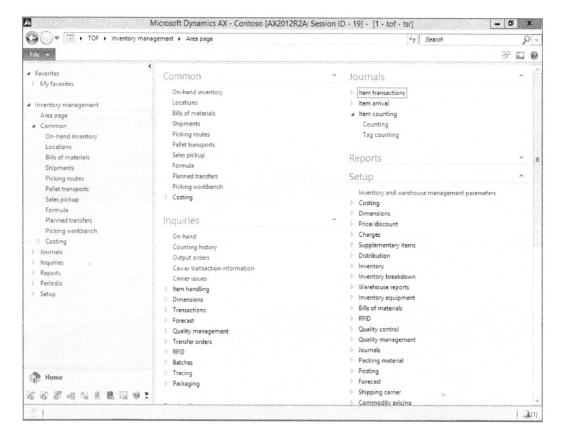

To do this, click on the **On Hand** menu item within the **Inquiries** grop of the **Inventory Management** area page.

Viewing On Hand Inventory

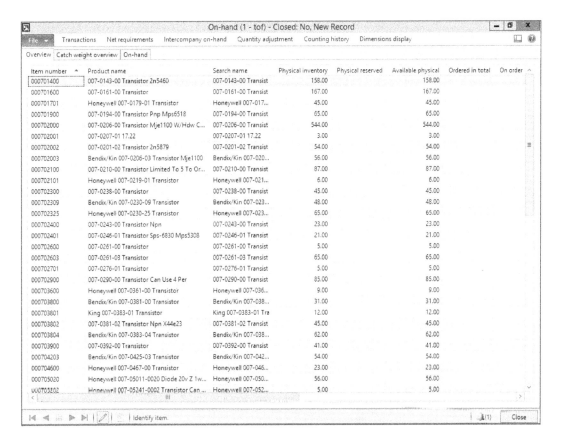

This will open up the **On Hand** inquiry. You won't see the locations, warehouse, or site though initially, but you can fix that by clicking on the **Dimension Display** button in the menu bar.

Viewing On Hand Inventory

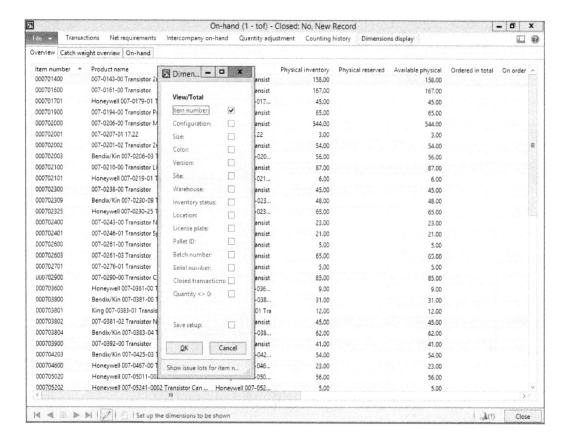

This will open up the inventory **Dimension** selector.

Viewing On Hand Inventory

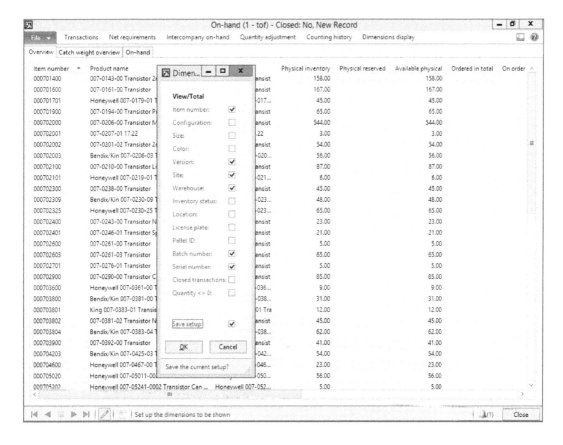

Click on the **Version**, **Site**, **Warehouse** and **Location** inventory dimensions, and then click on the **Save Setup** flag to make this the standard for the form and then click the **OK** button.

Viewing On Hand Inventory

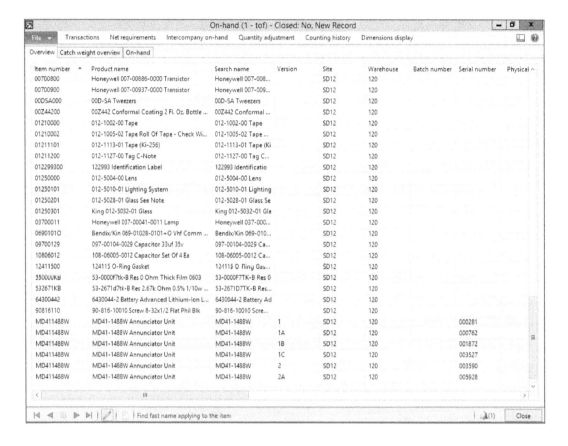

When you return back to the **On Hand** inquiry, now you will see where all of the products are.

That's much better.

Performing A Manual Count Adjustment

Sometimes you might find that you need to quickly perform a cycle count adjustment for a single product. You can go through the full cycle count generation if you like, but if you want there is another option for you, and that is to perform a quantity adjustment directly from the inventory inquiry itself.

Performing A Manual Count Adjustment

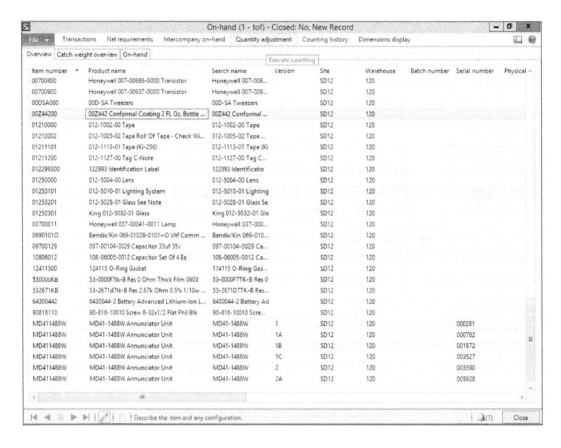

To do this all you need to do is select the item that you want to adjust from within the **On Hand** inquiry and then click on the **Quantity Adjustment** button in the menu bar.

Performing A Manual Count Adjustment

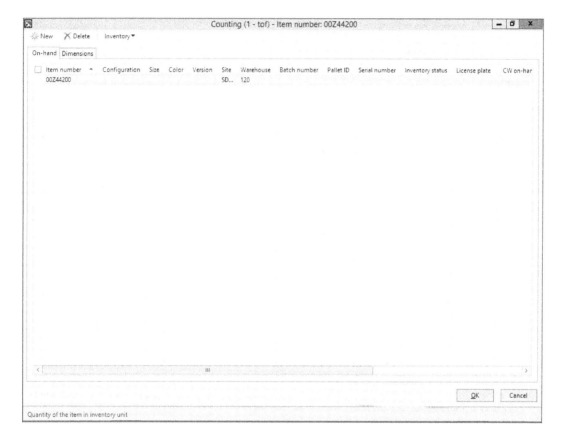

This will open up a little mini count for you just for that product.

Performing A Manual Count Adjustment

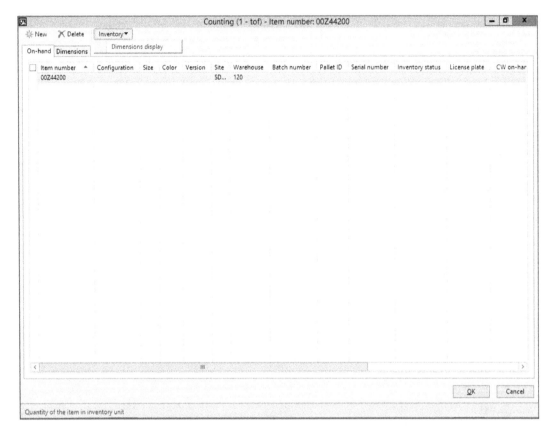

For this form, the first time that we come in we are actually seeing more dimensions than we want so click on the **Dimensions** button in the menu bar and select the **Dimension Display** menu item.

Performing A Manual Count Adjustment

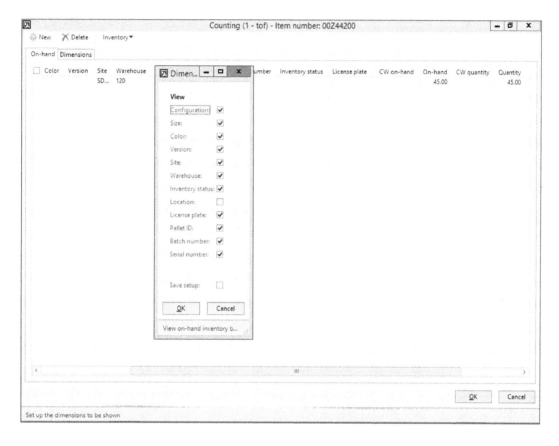

When the inventory **Dimension** list is displayed we will see that almost all of the dimensions are selected.

Performing A Manual Count Adjustment

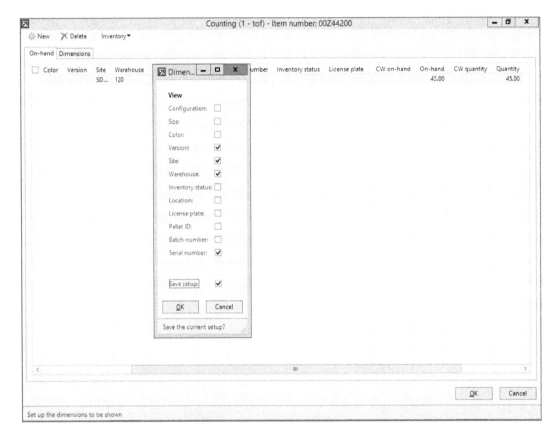

Unselect all but the **Version**, **Warehouse**, **Location**, and **Serial Number** and then click on the **Save Setup** flag to make this the form default. Then click on the **OK** button.

Performing A Manual Count Adjustment

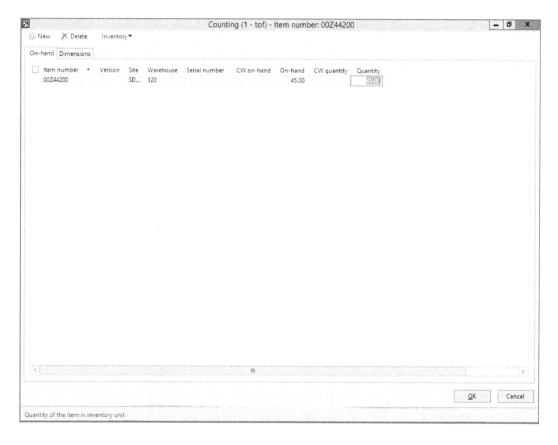

Now we will see the current count quantity for the item.

Performing A Manual Count Adjustment

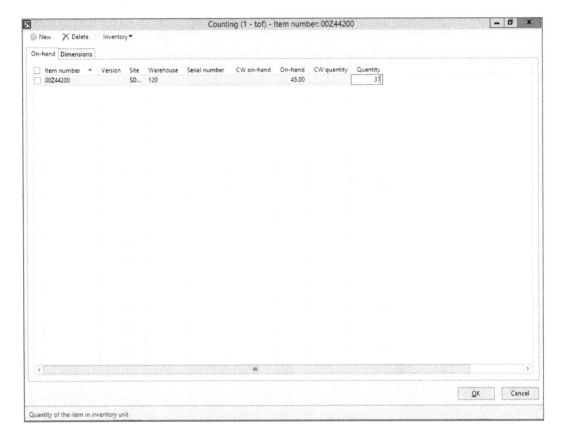

To adjust the item quantity, just change the **Quantity** value and then click on the **OK** button.

Performing A Manual Count Adjustment

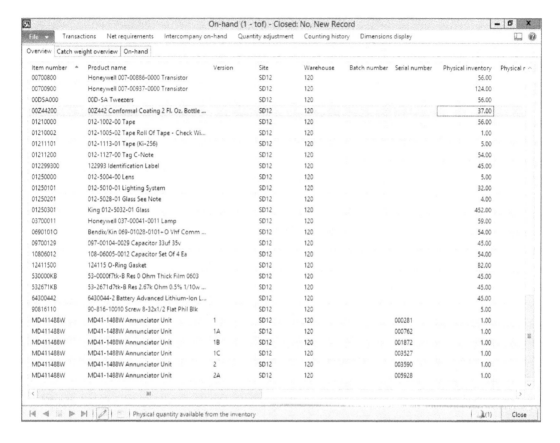

That will perform the adjustment for you and when you return to the **On Hand** inquiry the inventory quantity will be updated.

Now that was too easy.

CONFIGURING BATCHED AND SERIALIZED PRODUCTS

If you want you can also track your products by batch or serial number within Dynamics AX. These are just extra inventory dimensions that you enable on your products and give you that extra level of traceability when you look at your products.

In this section we will show you how to configure the batch and serial numbers and how to use them with products.

Configuring Number Groups

Before we start though there is just one small setup step that we need to perform, and that is to set up some **Number Groups**. These are used to control how the batch and serial numbers are tracked against a product.

Configuring Number Groups

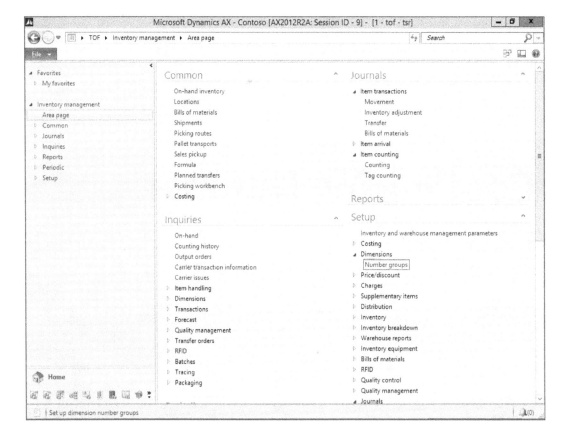

To do this, click on the **Number Groups** menu item within the **Dimensions** folder of the **Setup** group within the **Inventory Management** area page.

Configuring Number Groups

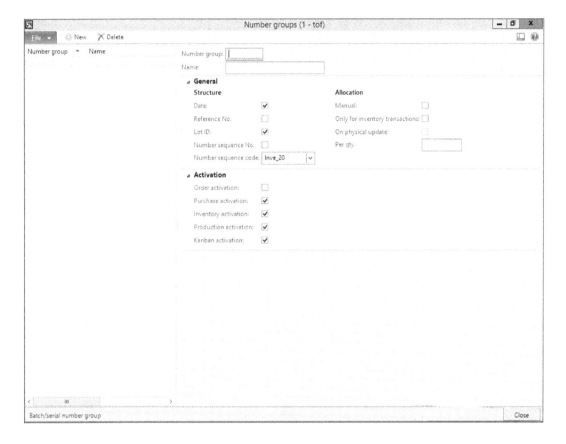

When the **Number Groups** maintenance form is displayed, click on the **New** button in the menu bar to create a new record.

Configuring Number Groups

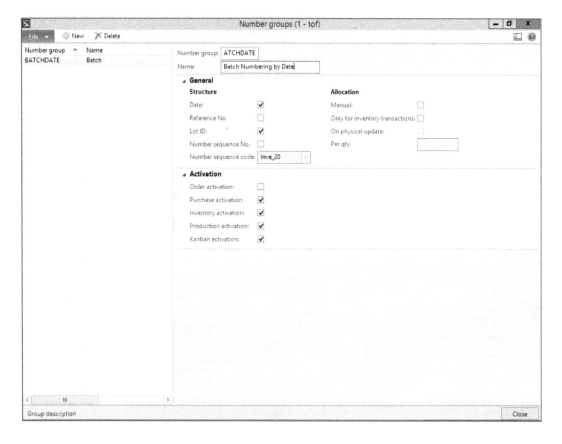

The first number group that we will create is will be to track batches, and will include the batch date. To do this, set the **Number Group** to **BATCHDATE** and the **Name** to **Batch Numbering By Date**.

Configuring Number Groups

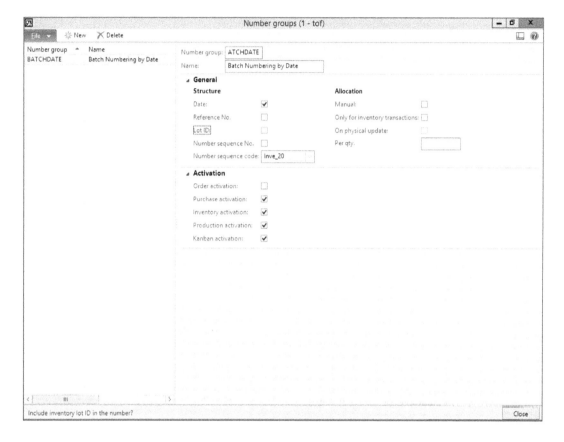

Uncheck the **Lot ID** flag.

Configuring Number Groups

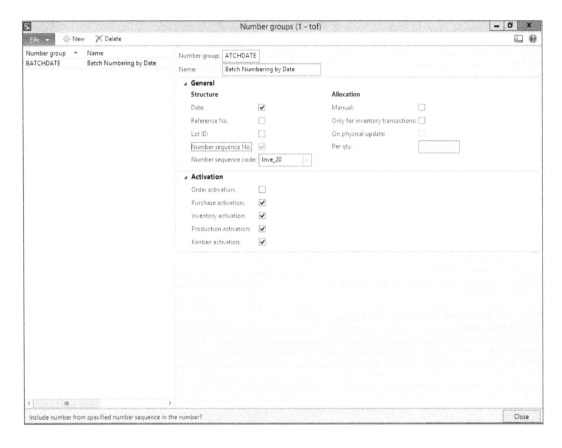

And check the **Number Sequence No.** which will tell the system to use the **Number Sequence Code** to create a new unique number that is appended to the date to make the unique lot number.

Configuring Number Groups

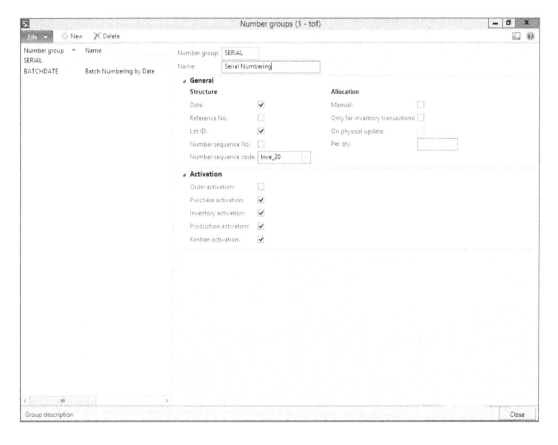

Now we will create another **Number Group** for the serialized products. To do this, click on the
New button in the menu bar to create a new record and set the **Number Group** to **SERIAL** and
the **Name** to **Serial Numbering**.

Configuring Number Groups

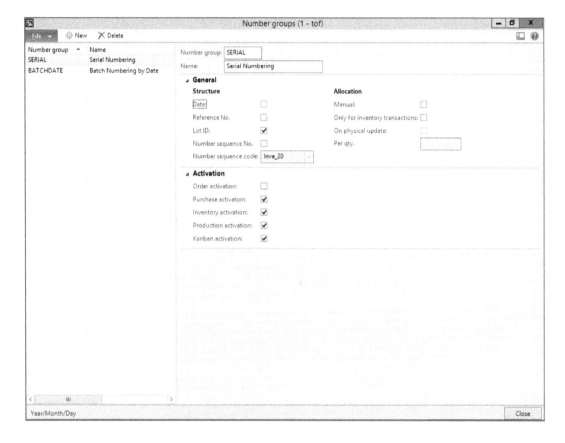

For the serial numbers, we just want them to be sequential, so uncheck the **Date** flag.

Configuring Number Groups

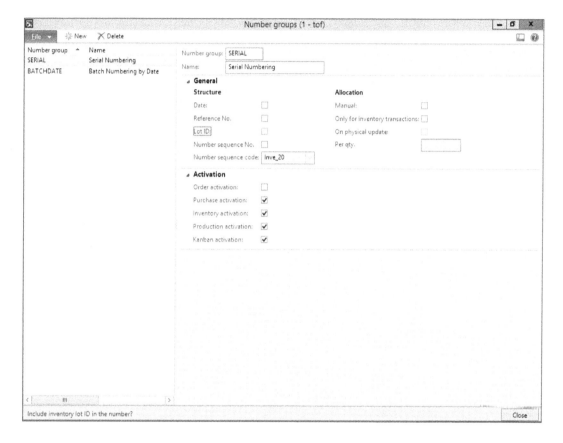

Also Uncheck the **Lot ID** flag.

Configuring Number Groups

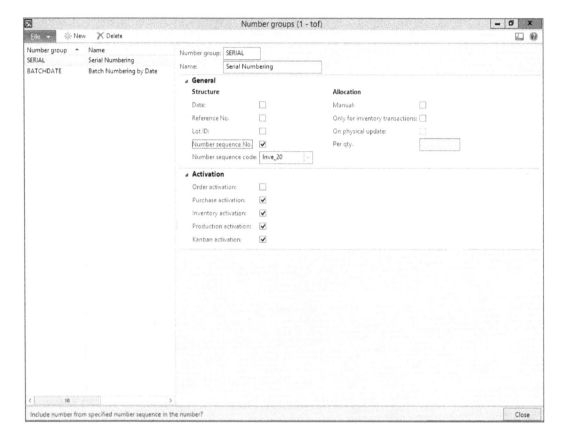

And then check the **Number Sequence No.** flag to use the **Number Sequence Code** to create the serial number.

Configuring Number Groups

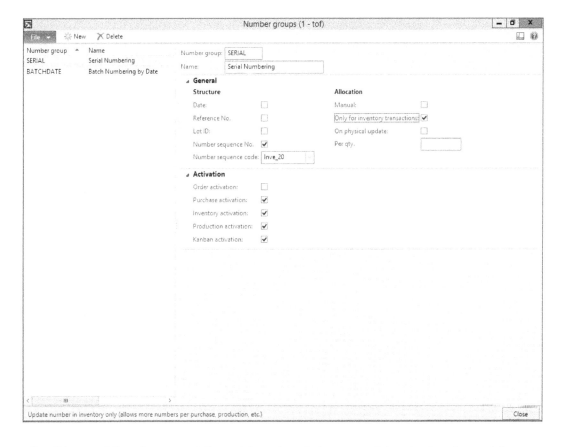

For this record though, we want the serial numbers to be sequential and unique for each item. To do this check the **Only for Inventory Transactions** flag within the **Allocation** field group.

Configuring Number Groups

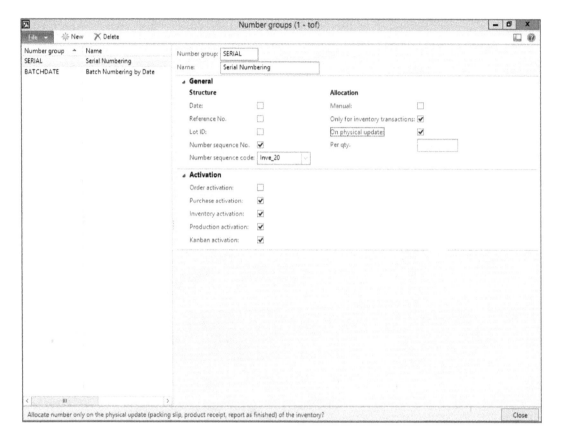

This will allow you to check the **Only Physical Update** flag.

Configuring Number Groups

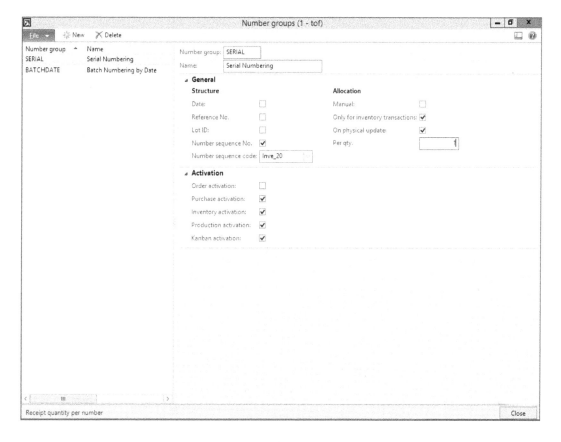

And then set the **Per Qty** to 1, which will tell the system to create a new serial number for each unit of 1.

You can create as many different batch and serial numbering formats as you want, and when you are done just click on the **Close** button to exit from the form.

Configuring A Batch Controlled Product

Now that we have a numbering group that will create our batch numbers for us, we can start using it on a product to have the system assign new batch numbers as the products are received in.

Configuring A Batch Controlled Product

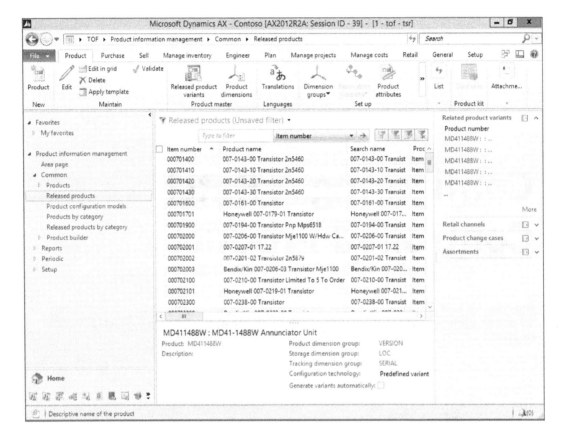

To do this, open up your released products list page and click on the **Product** button within the **New** group of the **Product** ribbon bat to create a new record.

Configuring A Batch Controlled Product

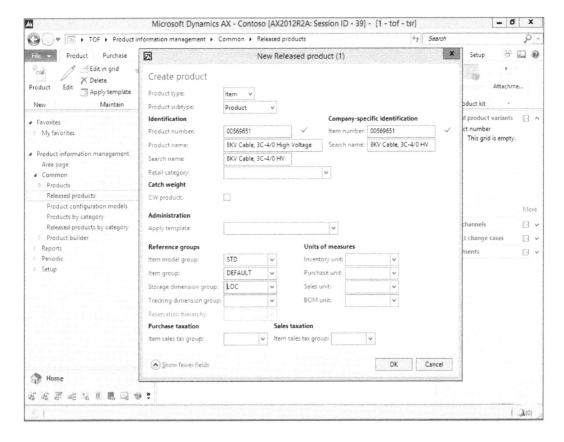

When the **New Released Product** dialog box is displayed, set up the product as you would normally do with a **Product Number**, **Product Name**, **Search Name**, **Item Model Group**, **Item Group**, and **Storage Dimension Group**.

Configuring A Batch Controlled Product

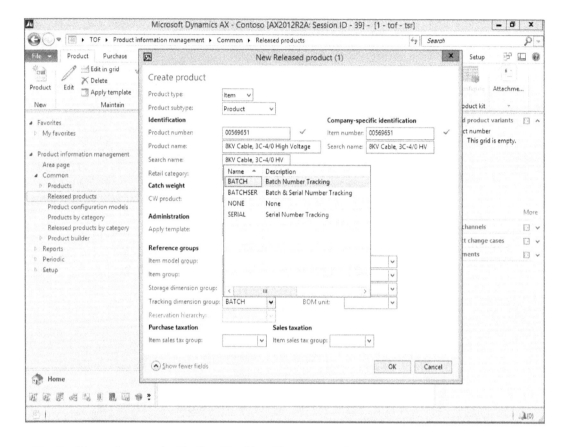

But for this product set the **Product Tracking Dimension** to be **BATCH**.

Configuring A Batch Controlled Product

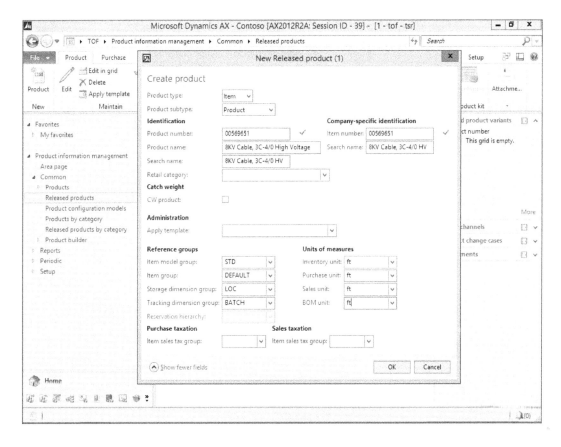

Finish off the template by setting the default **Units Of Measure** and then click the **OK** button.

Configuring A Batch Controlled Product

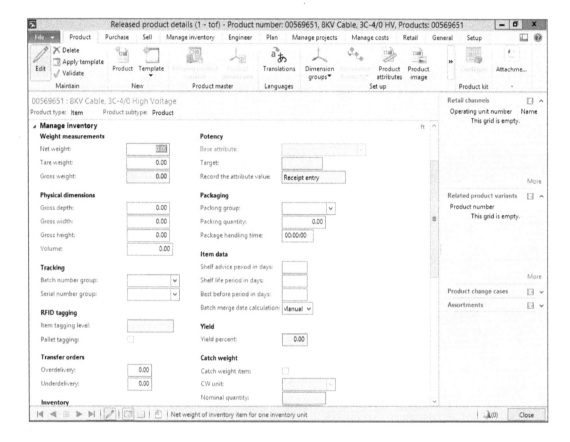

Open up the product that you just created and expand out the **Manage Inventory** tab group.

Configuring A Batch Controlled Product

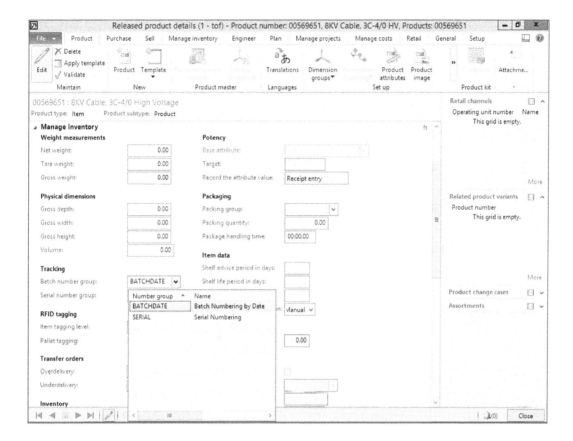

Within the **Tracking** field group, click on the **Batch Number Group** dropdown list and select the **BATCHDATE** number group that you just created.

Then tidy up the setup of the product by updating all of the costs, prices, and perform a cost activation.

Configuring A Batch Controlled Product

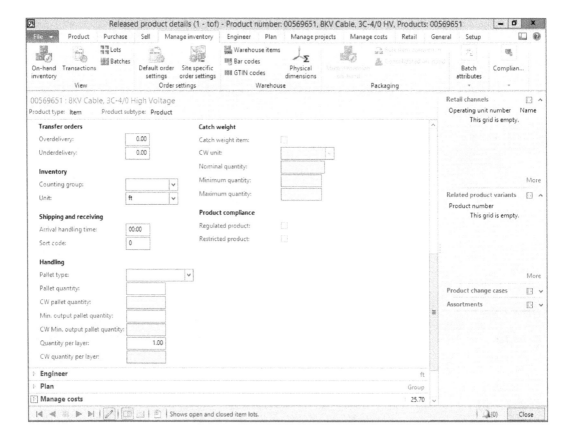

Once your product is configured you can see the batch numbers in action by creating some inventory. A quick way to do this from the product itself is to click on the **On Hand Inventory** button within the **View** group of the **Manage Inventory** ribbon bar.

Configuring A Batch Controlled Product

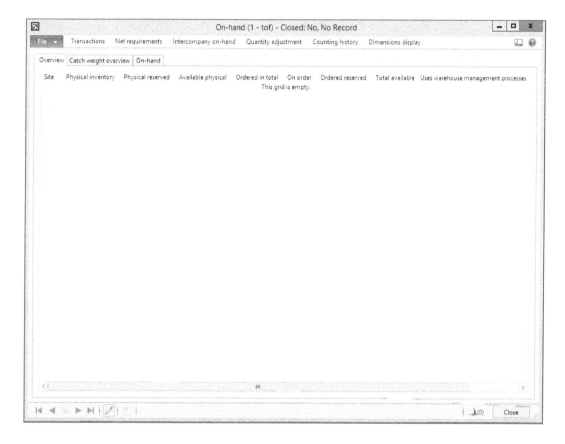

This will show you all of the inventory that you have on hand – which is nothing right now. To add some inventory, just click on the **Quantity Adjustment** button in the menu bar to perform an ad-hoc count.

Configuring A Batch Controlled Product

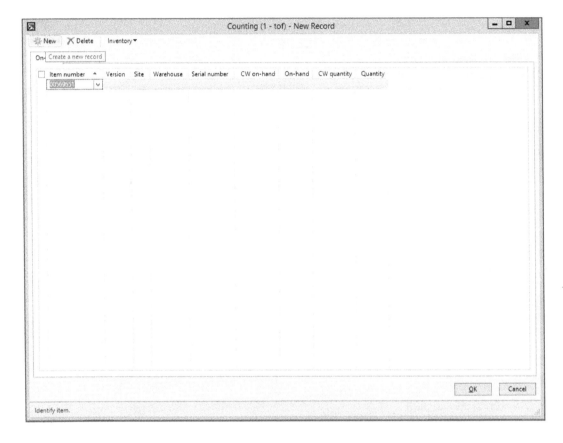

When the **Counting** form is displayed, click on the **New** button to create a new count record.

Configuring A Batch Controlled Product

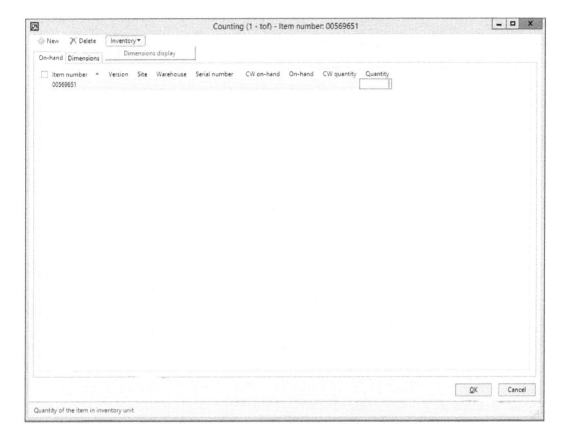

By default you don't see many of the inventory dimensions on this form, so to fix that, click on the **Inventory** button in the menu bar and select the **Dimension Display** menu item.

Configuring A Batch Controlled Product

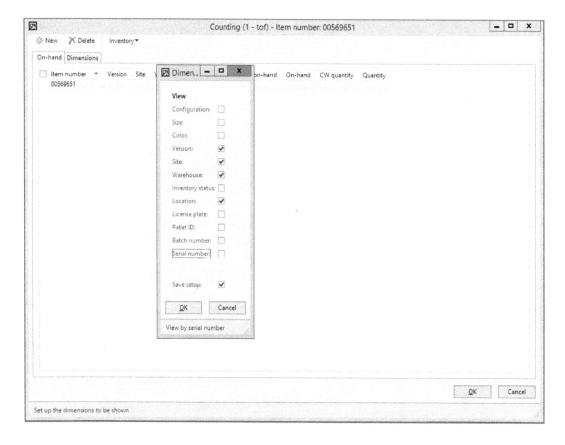

When the inventory **Dimensions** selector is displayed, you will see that the **Batch Number** and **Serial Number** dimensions are not enabled.

Configuring A Batch Controlled Product

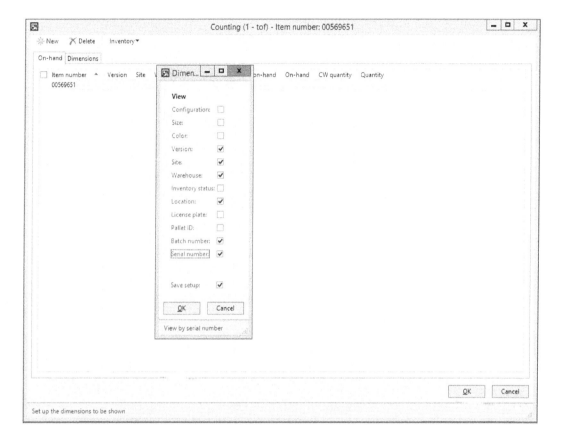

So check the **Batch Number** and **Serial Number** flags and click on the **OK** button.

Configuring A Batch Controlled Product

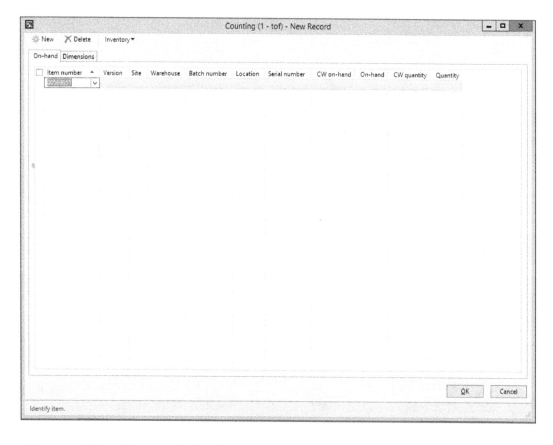

Now you will be able to see the batch and serial fields.

Configuring A Batch Controlled Product

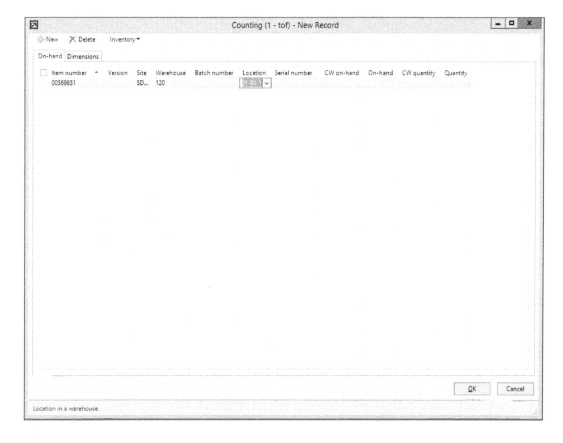

Set the **Site** to **SD12**, the **Warehouse** to **120**, and the **Location** to **01-01-1**. Don't assign a batch number though for this example because the numbering in this case is automatic.

Configuring A Batch Controlled Product

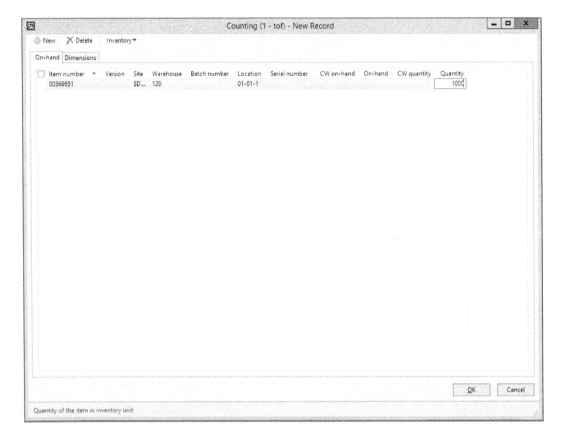

Then set the **Quantity** to **1000** and click on the **OK** button.

Configuring A Batch Controlled Product

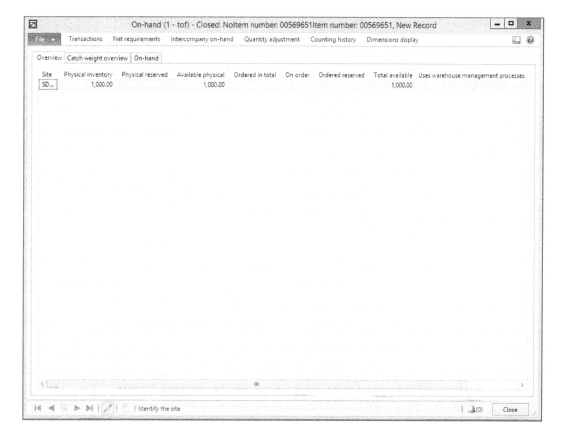

When you return back to the **On Hand Inquiry** you will see that the inventory has been created.

Configuring A Batch Controlled Product

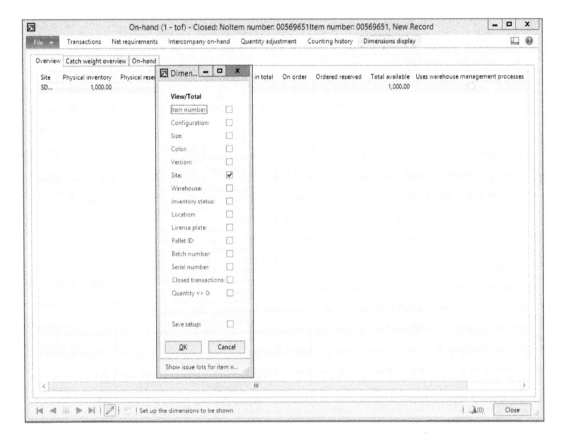

The only problem is that we can't see the dimensions. To fix that, click on the **Dimension Display** button in the menu bar to open up the Inventory **Dimension** dialog.

Configuring A Batch Controlled Product

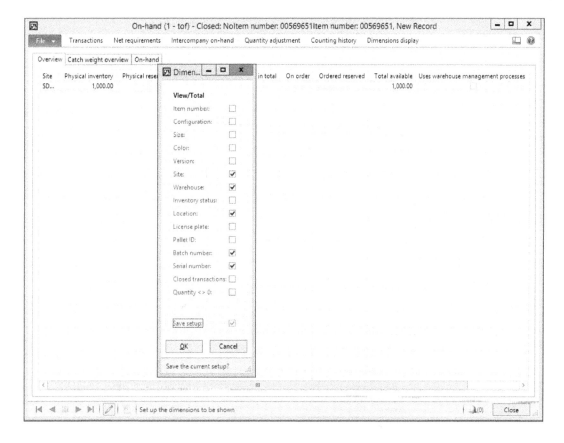

Check the **Site**, **Warehouse**, **Location**, **Batch Number**, and **Serial Number** flags. Then check the **Save Setup** flag to make this the default view and then click on the **OK** button.

Configuring A Batch Controlled Product

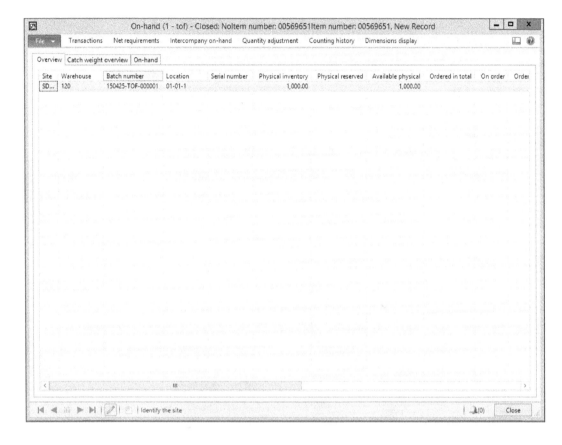

Now when you look at the inventory on hand you will see that the **Batch Number** has been automatically assigned to our product.

How cool is that?

Viewing Batch Details

There is another way that you can view the batch details, and that is directly through the **Released Product** details page.

Viewing Batch Details

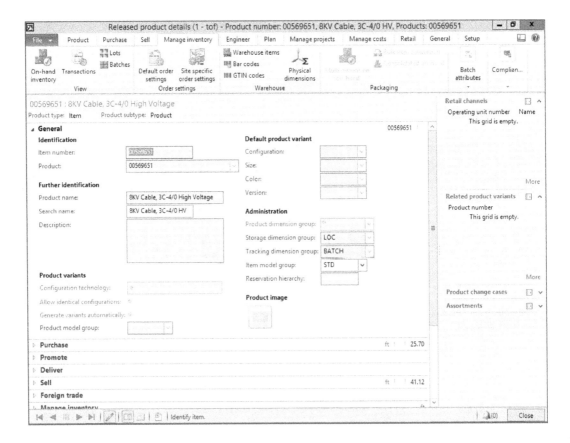

To do this, just open up your batch controlled product through the **Released Products Details** form and click on the **Batches** menu item within the **View** group of the **Manage Inventory** ribbon bar.

Viewing Batch Details

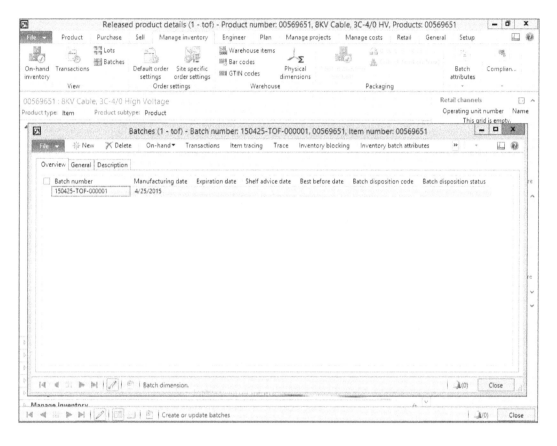

This will open up a list of all of the batches that you have created for this product. Notice also that the batches are date controlled and through here you are also able to update the **Expiration Dates**.

When you are done, just click on the **Close** button to exit from the form.

Configuring A Serialized Product

Additionally you can create products that are serialized.

Configuring A Serialized Product

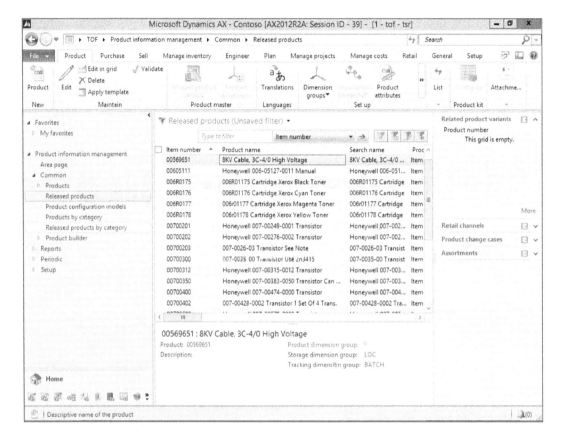

To do this, open up your released products list page and click on the **Product** button within the **New** group of the **Product** ribbon bat to create a new record.

Configuring A Serialized Product

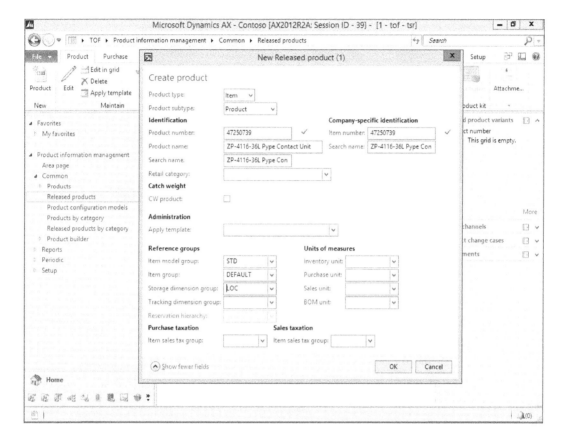

When the **New Released Product** dialog box is displayed, set up the product as you would normally do with a **Product Number**, **Product Name**, **Search Name**, **Item Model Group**, **Item Group**, and **Storage Dimension Group**.

Configuring A Serialized Product

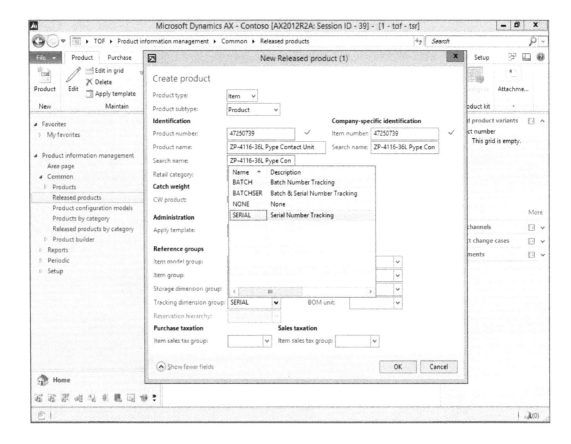

For this product set the **Product Tracking Dimension** to be **SERIAL**.

Configuring A Serialized Product

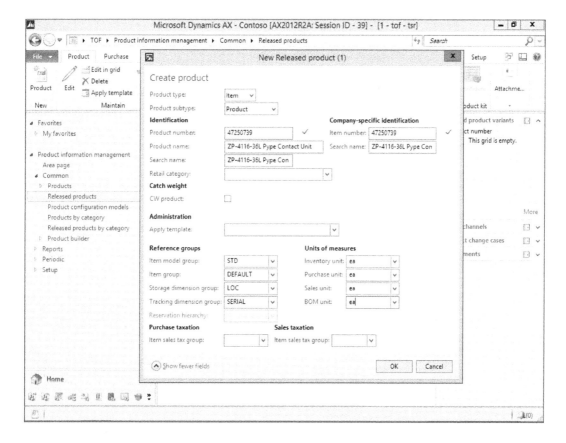

Finish off the template by setting the default **Units Of Measure** and then click the **OK** button.

Configuring A Serialized Product

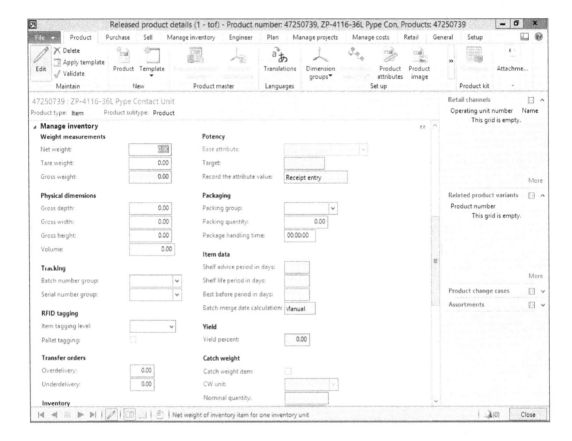

Open up the product that you just created and expand out the **Manage Inventory** tab group.

Configuring A Serialized Product

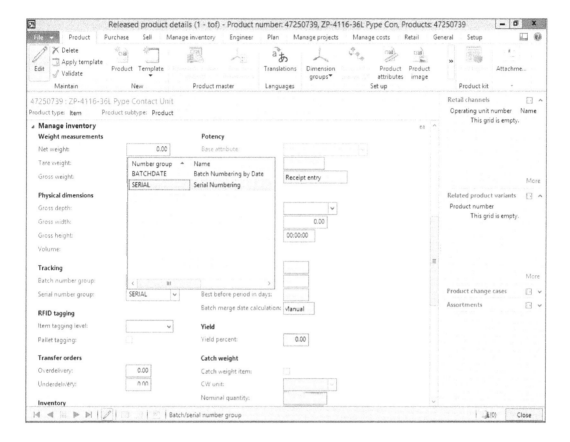

Within the **Tracking** field group, click on the **Serial Number Group** dropdown list and select the **SERIAL** number group that you just created.

Then tidy up the setup of the product by updating all of the costs, prices, and perform a cost activation.

Configuring A Serialized Product

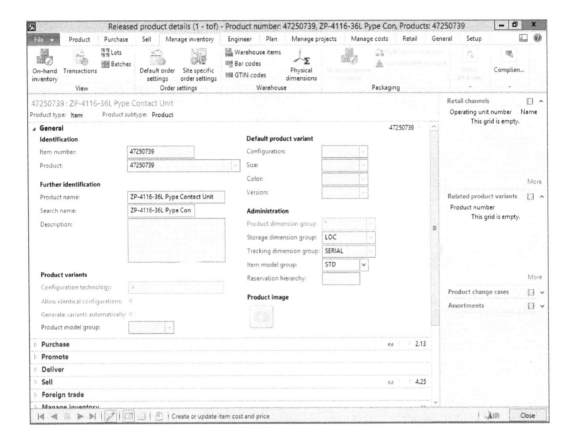

Now that the product is configured you can see the serial numbers in action by creating some more inventory by clicking on the **On Hand Inventory** button within the **View** group of the **Manage Inventory** ribbon bar.

Configuring A Serialized Product

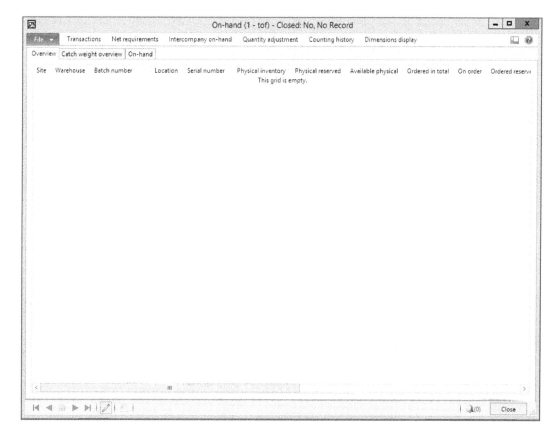

This will show you all of the inventory that you have on hand – which is nothing right now. To add some inventory, just click on the **Quantity Adjustment** button in the menu bar to perform an ad-hoc count.

Configuring A Serialized Product

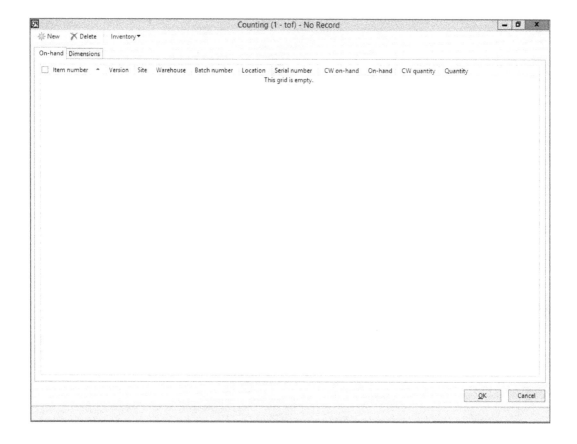

Configuring A Serialized Product

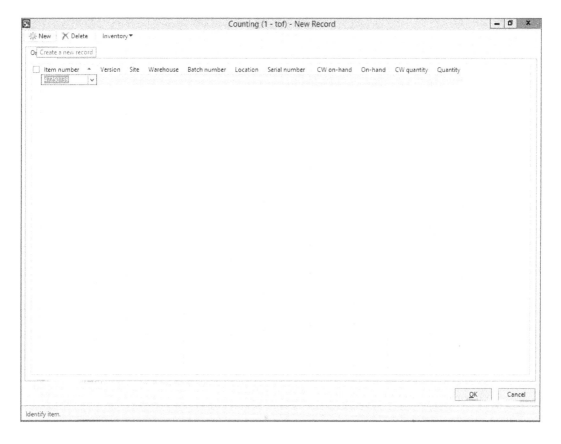

When the **Counting** form is displayed, click on the **New** button in the menu bar to create a new record.

Configuring A Serialized Product

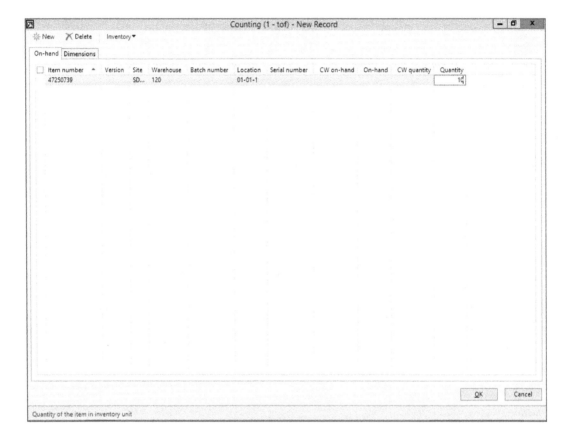

Then set the **Site** to be **SD12**, the **Warehouse** to **120**, and the **Location** to **01-01-1**. Then set the **Quantity** to **10.**

Notice that we do not specify the **Serial Number** because it is set to auto generate.

When you have done that, just click on the **OK** button.

Configuring A Serialized Product

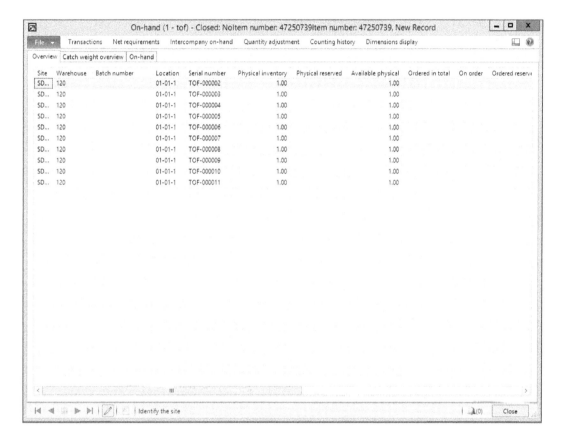

When you return back to the **On Hand** inquiry you will see that 10 serial numbers have been automatically created for you.

That was easy.

SUMMARY

Hopefully this guide has given you a good foundation of knowledge of how the Inventory Management area of Dynamics AX works, and also some of the key features that are available for you that allow you to configure your inventory controls, structure your inventory locations and also update your products to enable them to be used within the Inventory Management area.

We are still just starting you off on your journey through Inventory Management though with this guide, and there is so much more that you can do within the Inventory Management area. So don't stop delving into this area because there is still so much more that you can take advantage of.

Want More Tips & Tricks For Dynamics AX?

The Tips & Tricks series is a compilation of all the cool things that I have found that you can do within Dynamics AX, and are also the basis for my Tips & Tricks presentations that I have been giving for the AXUG, and online. Unfortunately book page size restrictions mean that I can only fit 50 tips & tricks per book, but I will create new volumes every time I reach the 50 Tip mark.

To get all of the details on this series, then here is the link:

http://dynamicsaxcompanions.com/tipsandtricks

Need More Help With Dynamics AX?

LUKE SKYWALKER MAY HAVE HAD THE FORCE,
BUT HE STILL NEEDED R2D2 TO PLOT THE
COURSE FOR HIM.
WHO IS YOUR COMPANION THAT WILL HELP YOU
NAVIGATE DYNAMICS AX?

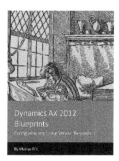

After creating a number of my walkthroughs on SlideShare showing how to configure the different areas within Dynamics AX, I had a lot of requests for the original documents so that people could get a better view of many of the screen shots and also have a easy reference as they worked through the same process within their own systems. To make them easier to access, I am in the process of moving all of the content to the Dynamics AX Companions website to easier access. If you are looking for details on how to configure and use Dynamics AX, then this is a great place for you to start.

Here is the link for the site:

http://dynamicsaxcompanions.com/

daxc

www.dynamicsaxcompanions.com

About Me

I am an author - I'm no Dan Brown but my books do contain a lot of secret codes and symbols that help guide you through the mysteries of Dynamics AX.

I am a curator - gathering all of the information that I can about Dynamics AX and filing it away within the Dynamics AX Companions archives.

I am a pitchman - I am forever extolling the virtues of Dynamics AX to the unwashed masses convincing them that it is the best ERP system in the world.

I am a Microsoft MVP - this is a big deal, there are less than 10 Dynamics AX MVP's in the US, and less than 30 worldwide.

I am a programmer - I know enough to get around within code, although I leave the hard stuff to the experts so save you all from my uncommented style.

WEB	www.murrayfife.me
	www.dynamicsaxcompanions.com
EMAIL	murray@dynamicsaxcompanions.com
TWITTER	@murrayfife
SKYPE	murrayfife
AMAZON	www.amazon.com/author/murrayfife

www.ingramcontent.com/pod-product-compliance
Lightning Source LLC
Chambersburg PA
CBHW080146060326
40689CB00018B/3865